CHARLES M. SCHULZ

SNOOPY'S LOVE BOOK

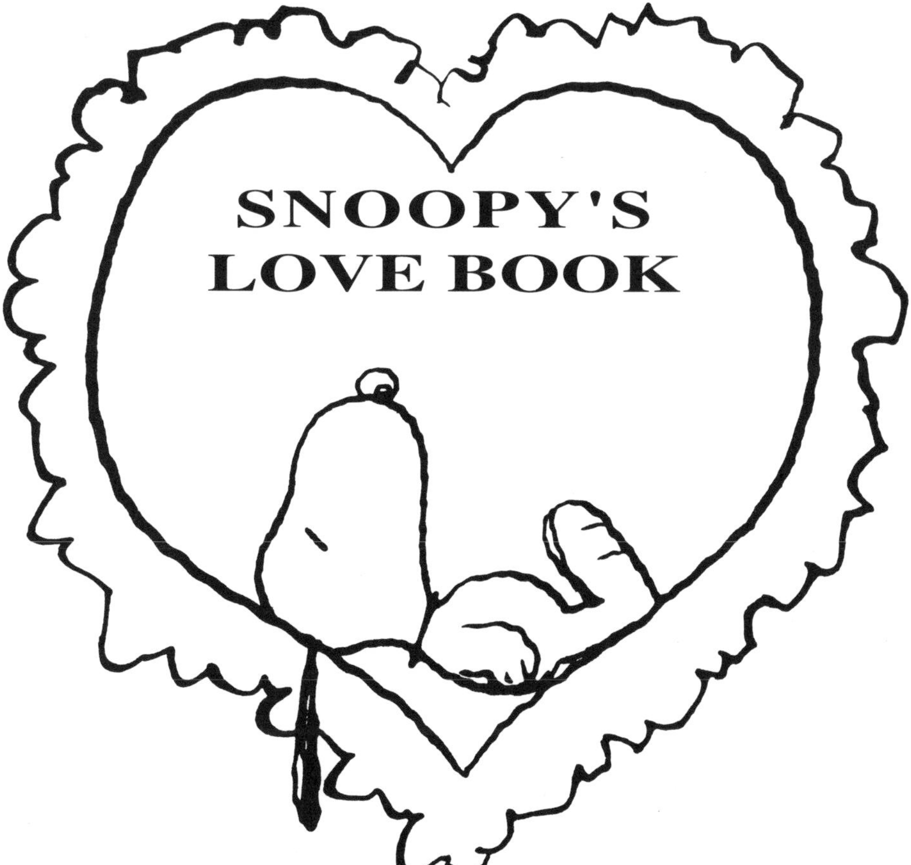

Henry Holt and Company
New York

YOU KNOW WHAT YOU SHOULD WRITE? YOU SHOULD WRITE A "KISS-AND-TELL" BOOK..
© 1988 United Feature Syndicate, Inc.
7-6
SMAK
I'M GONNA TELL! I'M GONNA TELL!
SCHULZ

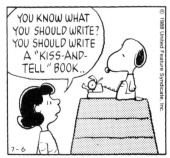

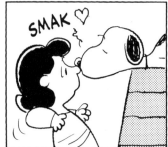

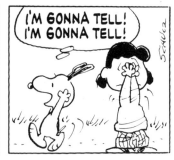

Henry Holt and Company, Inc.
Publishers since 1866
115 West 18th Street
New York, New York 10011

Henry Holt ® is a registered trademark of Henry Holt and Company, Inc.

Published in Canada by Fitzhenry & Whiteside Ltd.,
195 Allstate Parkway, Markham, Ontario L3R 4T8.

Library of Congress Catalog Card Number: 93-61350

ISBN 0-8050-3146-4

Henry Holt books are available for special promotions and premiums.
For details contact: Director, Special Markets.

First Edition — 1994

Printed in the United States of America
All first editions are printed on acid-free paper. ∞

1 3 5 7 9 10 8 6 4 2

SNOOPY'S LOVE BOOK

CONTENTS

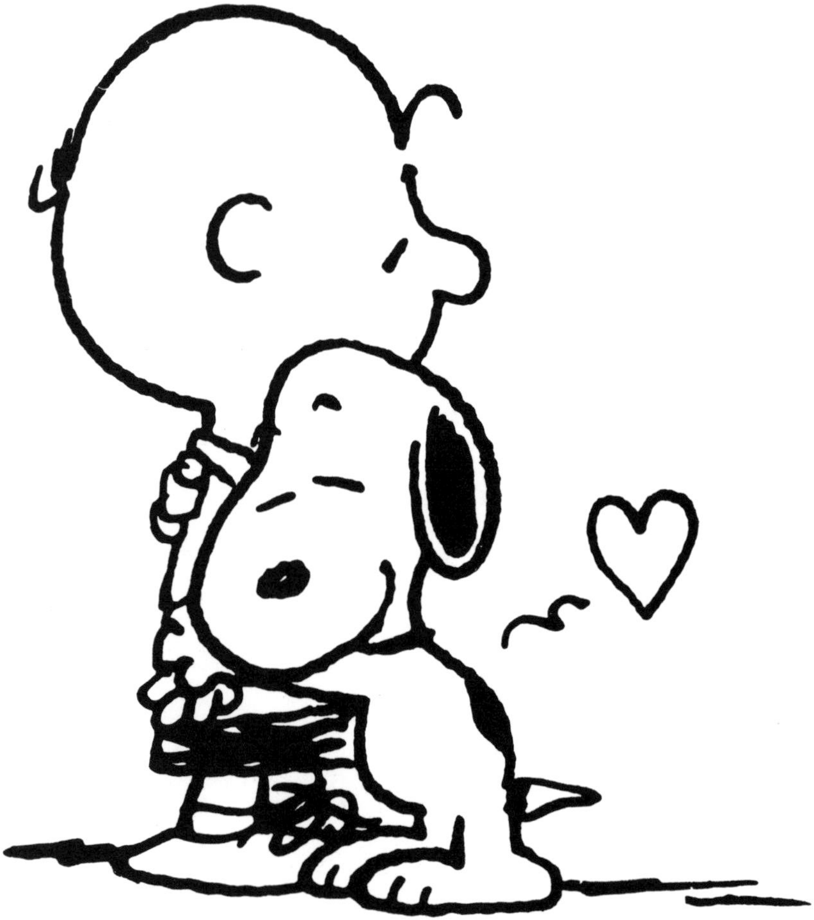

DEAREST DARLING

When I was in the first grade, the teacher put a valentine box on a table in front of the room. It was two days before Valentine's Day and we were to bring to school the cards we wanted to give the kids we liked. Obviously, there were some kids I liked more than others, but because I didn't wish to offend anyone, I made out a list that included everyone. My mother helped me select all the cards, and I took them to school the next day. Classrooms are pretty big to a first grader, and it was a long walk from where I sat up to the front of the room where the valentine box waited. Everyone could watch as you walked to the front of the room and dropped each card through the slit on top of the box. I couldn't do it. I took all the valentines home.

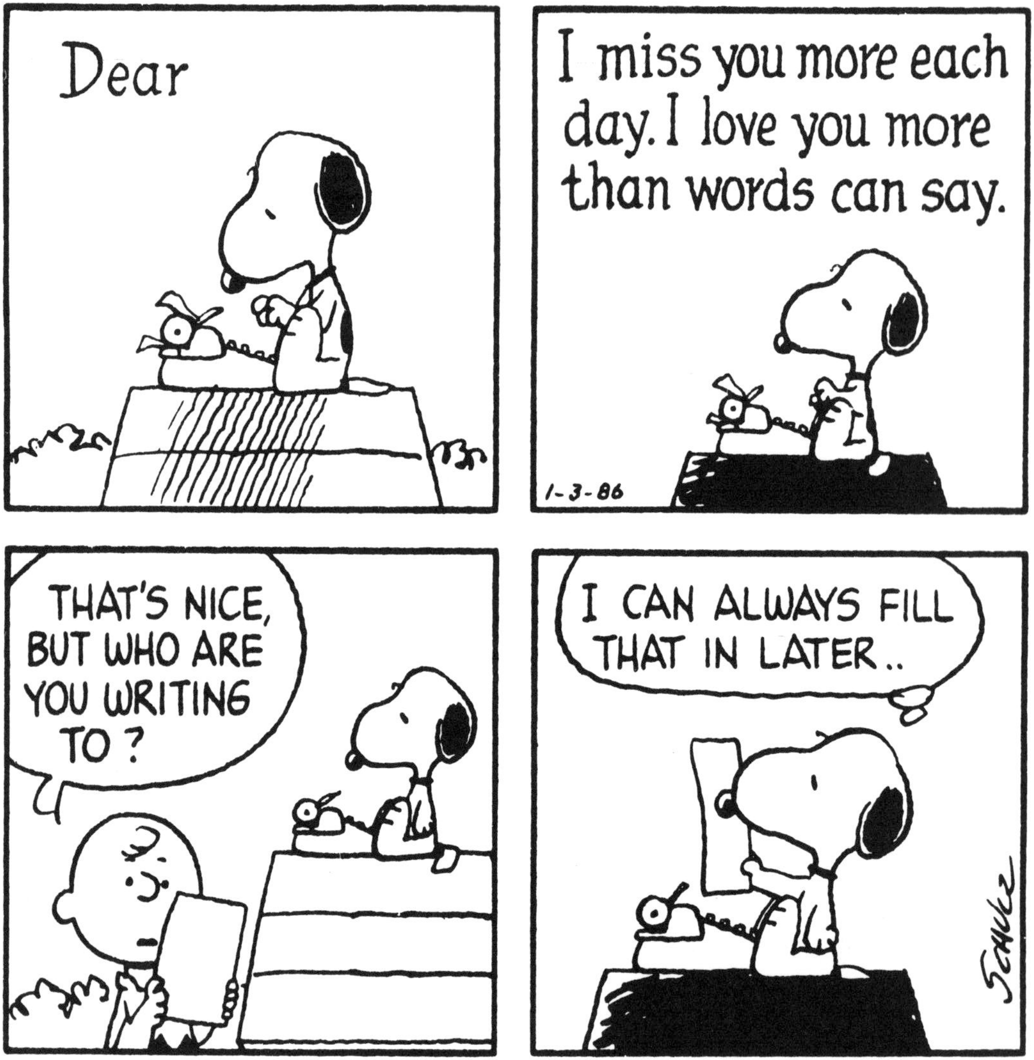
Dear
I miss you more each day. I love you more than words can say.
1-3-86
THAT'S NICE, BUT WHO ARE YOU WRITING TO ?
I CAN ALWAYS FILL THAT IN LATER..
SCHULZ

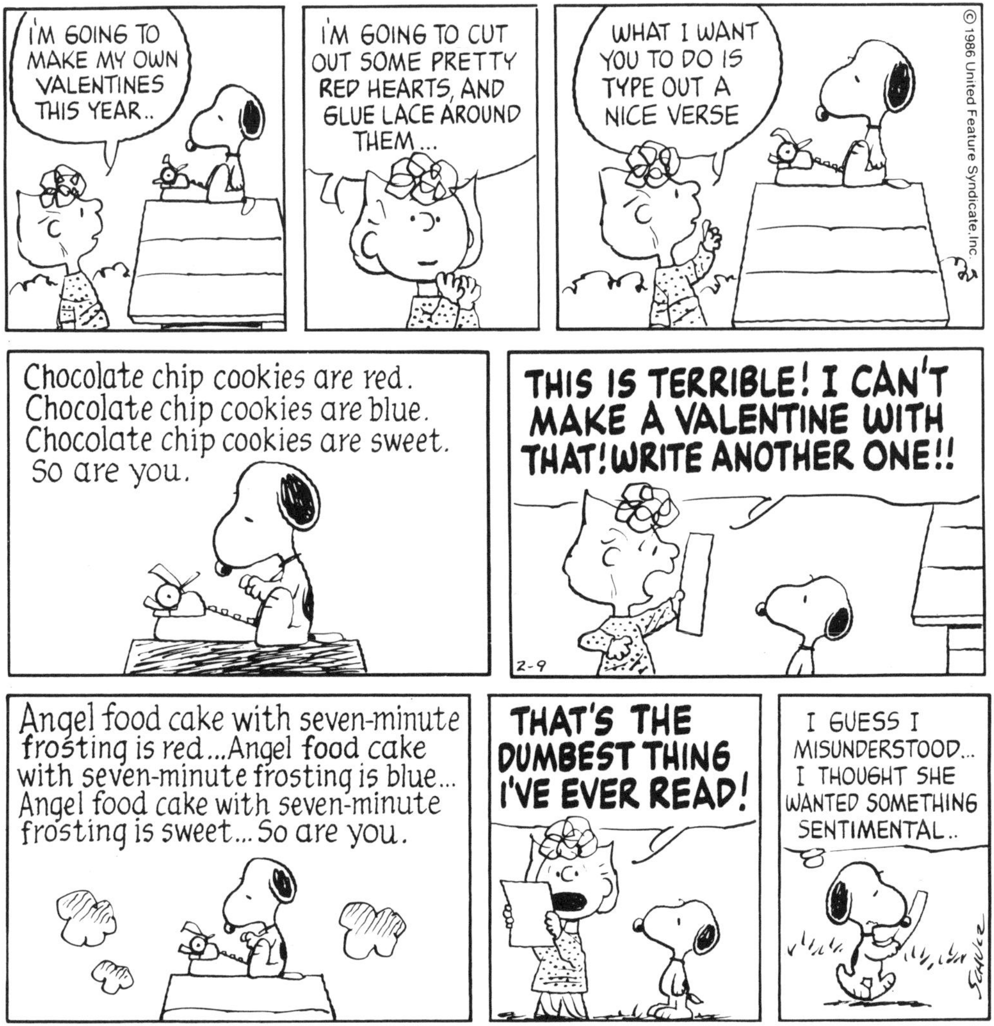
I'M GOING TO MAKE MY OWN VALENTINES THIS YEAR..
I'M GOING TO CUT OUT SOME PRETTY RED HEARTS, AND GLUE LACE AROUND THEM...
WHAT I WANT YOU TO DO IS TYPE OUT A NICE VERSE
© 1986 United Feature Syndicate, Inc.
Chocolate chip cookies are red. Chocolate chip cookies are blue. Chocolate chip cookies are sweet. So are you.
THIS IS TERRIBLE! I CAN'T MAKE A VALENTINE WITH THAT! WRITE ANOTHER ONE!!
2-9
Angel food cake with seven-minute frosting is red...Angel food cake with seven-minute frosting is blue... Angel food cake with seven-minute frosting is sweet...So are you.
THAT'S THE DUMBEST THING I'VE EVER READ!
I GUESS I MISUNDERSTOOD... I THOUGHT SHE WANTED SOMETHING SENTIMENTAL..
SCHULZ

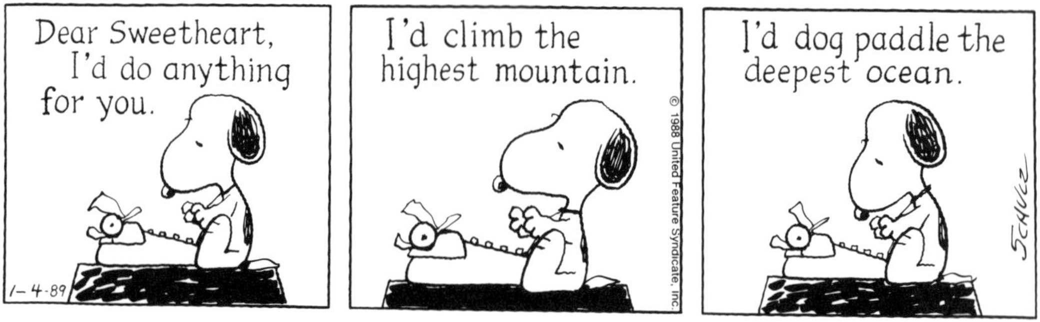
Dear Sweetheart,
I'd do anything for you.
1-4-89
I'd climb the highest mountain.
© 1988 United Feature Syndicate, Inc.
I'd dog paddle the deepest ocean.
SCHULZ

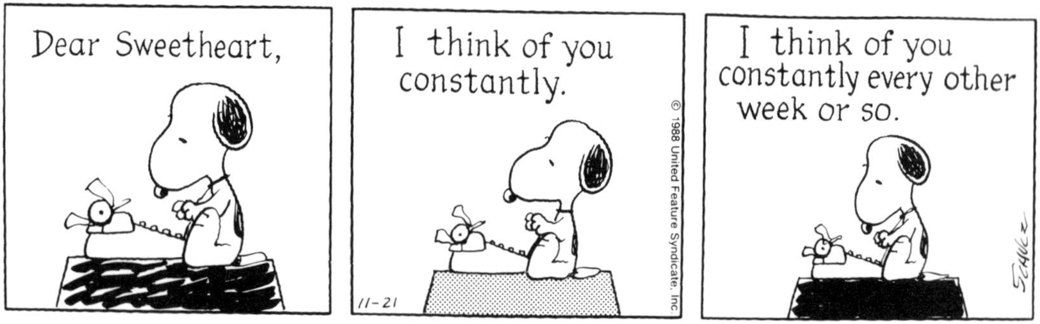
Dear Sweetheart,
I think of you constantly.
11-21
© 1988 United Feature Syndicate, Inc.
I think of you constantly every other week or so.
SCHULZ

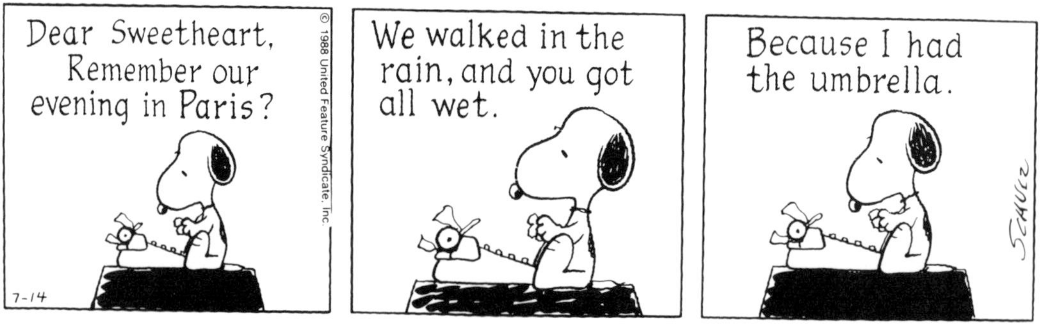
Dear Sweetheart,
Remember our evening in Paris?
7-14
© 1988 United Feature Syndicate, Inc.
We walked in the rain, and you got all wet.
Because I had the umbrella.
SCHULZ

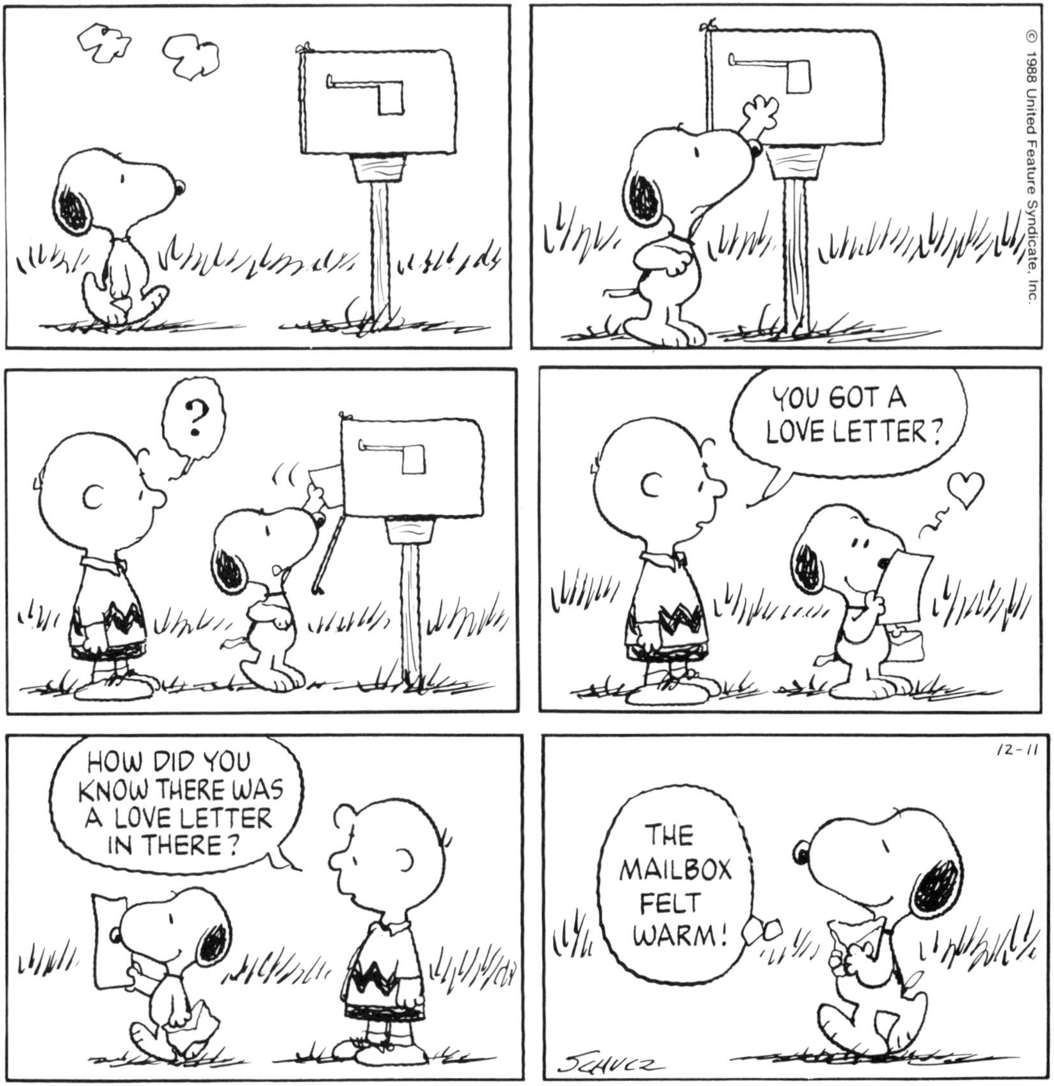
© 1988 United Feature Syndicate, Inc.
?
YOU GOT A LOVE LETTER?
HOW DID YOU KNOW THERE WAS A LOVE LETTER IN THERE?
12-11
THE MAILBOX FELT WARM!
SCHULZ

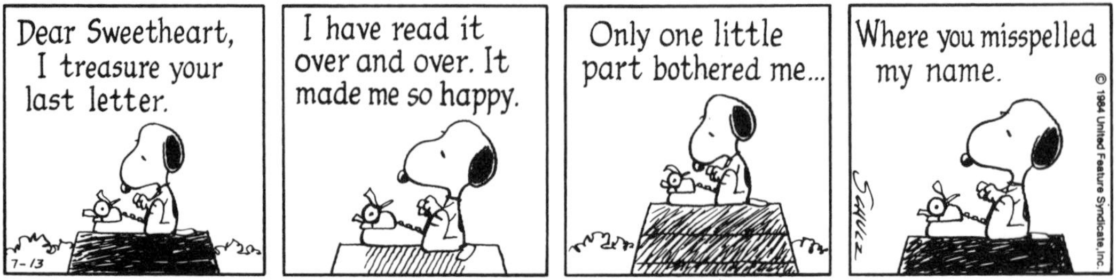
Dear Sweetheart, I treasure your last letter.
7-13
I have read it over and over. It made me so happy.
Only one little part bothered me...
Where you misspelled my name.
SCHULZ
© 1984 United Feature Syndicate, Inc.

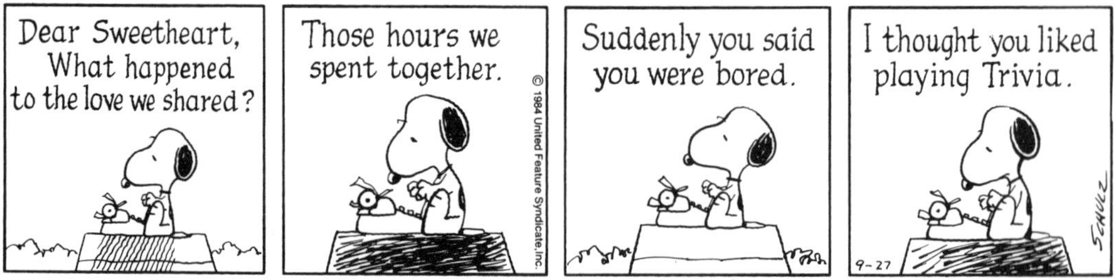
Dear Sweetheart, What happened to the love we shared?
Those hours we spent together.
© 1984 United Feature Syndicate, Inc.
Suddenly you said you were bored.
I thought you liked playing Trivia.
SCHULZ
9-27

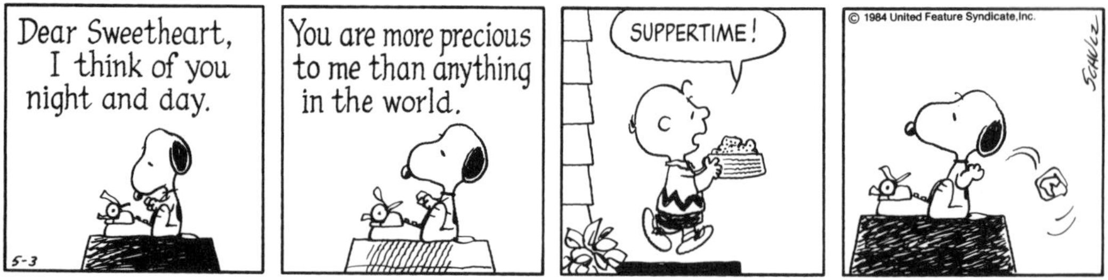
Dear Sweetheart, I think of you night and day.
5-3
You are more precious to me than anything in the world.
SUPPERTIME!
© 1984 United Feature Syndicate, Inc.
SCHULZ

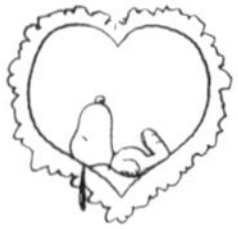

WAITING, WAITING

I don't know why there's so much unrequited love in my strip. I seem to be fascinated by unrequited love, if not obsessed by it: Sally loves Linus, Linus can't stand her; Lucy loves Schroeder, Schroeder can't stand her; Charlie Brown loves the red-haired girl, but doesn't even dare to get near her. There's something funny about unrequited love — I suppose it's because we can all identify with it. We've all been turned down by somebody we love, and it's probably the most bitter blow in life.

11

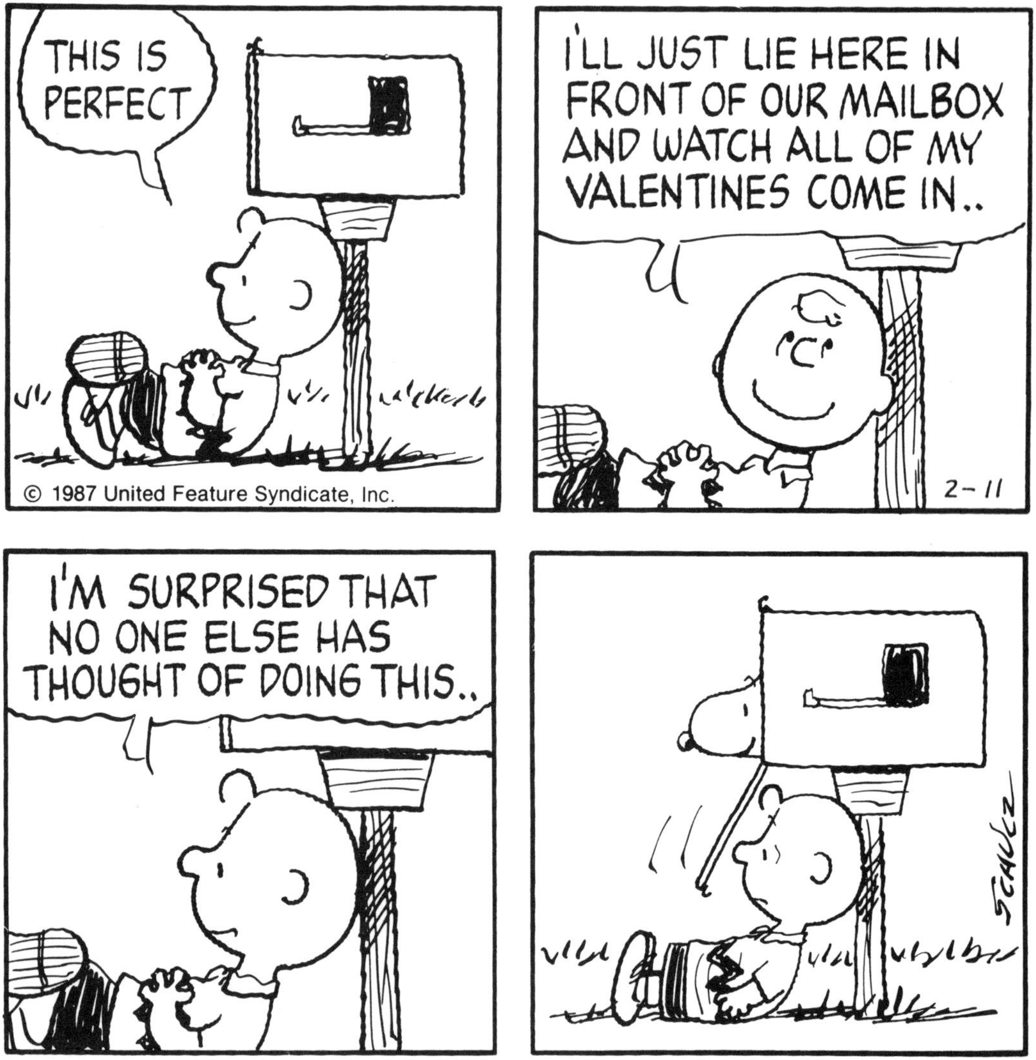
THIS IS PERFECT
© 1987 United Feature Syndicate, Inc.
I'LL JUST LIE HERE IN FRONT OF OUR MAILBOX AND WATCH ALL OF MY VALENTINES COME IN..
2-11
I'M SURPRISED THAT NO ONE ELSE HAS THOUGHT OF DOING THIS..
SCHULZ

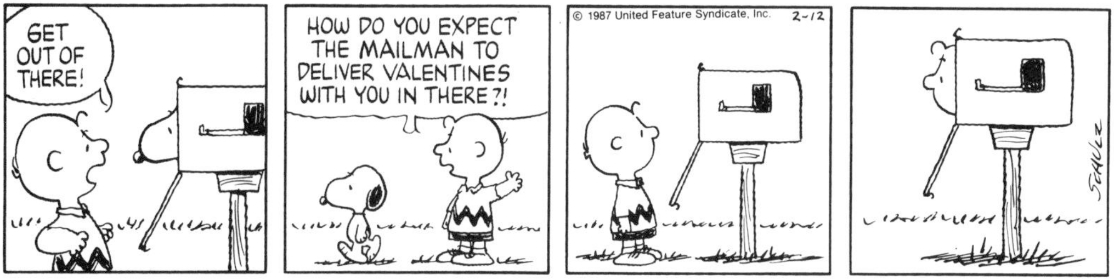
GET OUT OF THERE!
HOW DO YOU EXPECT THE MAILMAN TO DELIVER VALENTINES WITH YOU IN THERE?!
© 1987 United Feature Syndicate, Inc.
2-12
SCHULZ

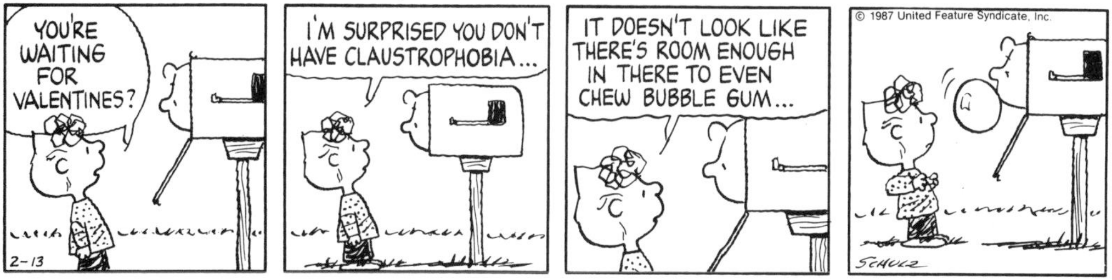
YOU'RE WAITING FOR VALENTINES?
2-13
I'M SURPRISED YOU DON'T HAVE CLAUSTROPHOBIA...
IT DOESN'T LOOK LIKE THERE'S ROOM ENOUGH IN THERE TO EVEN CHEW BUBBLE GUM...
© 1987 United Feature Syndicate, Inc.
SCHULZ

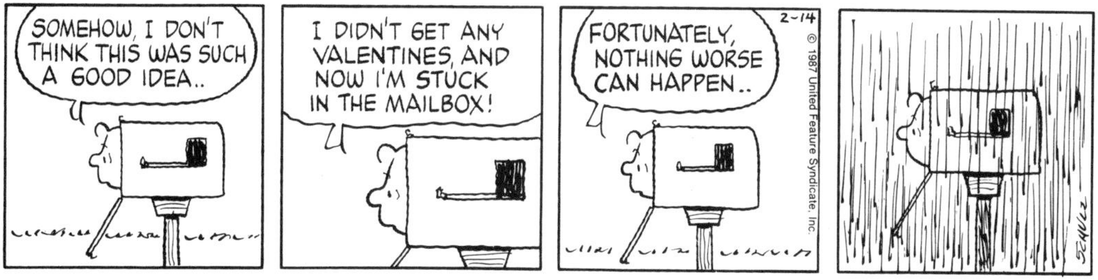
SOMEHOW, I DON'T THINK THIS WAS SUCH A GOOD IDEA..
I DIDN'T GET ANY VALENTINES, AND NOW I'M STUCK IN THE MAILBOX!
2-14
FORTUNATELY, NOTHING WORSE CAN HAPPEN..
© 1987 United Feature Syndicate, Inc.
SCHULZ

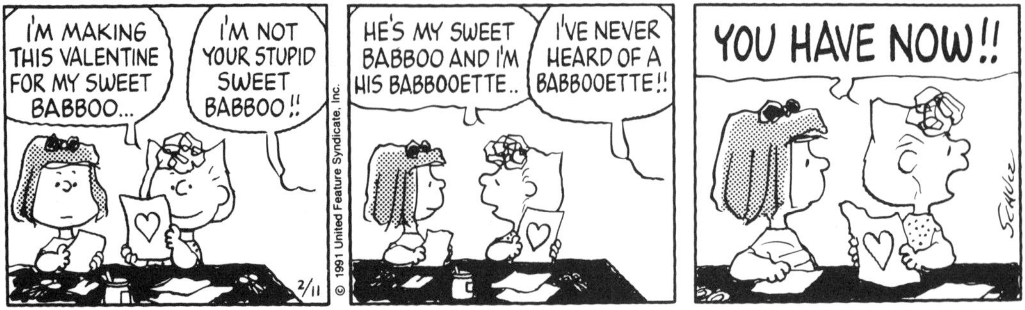
I'M MAKING THIS VALENTINE FOR MY SWEET BABBOO...
I'M NOT YOUR STUPID SWEET BABBOO!!
2/11
© 1991 United Feature Syndicate, Inc.
HE'S MY SWEET BABBOO AND I'M HIS BABBOOETTE..
I'VE NEVER HEARD OF A BABBOOETTE!!
YOU HAVE NOW!!
SCHULZ

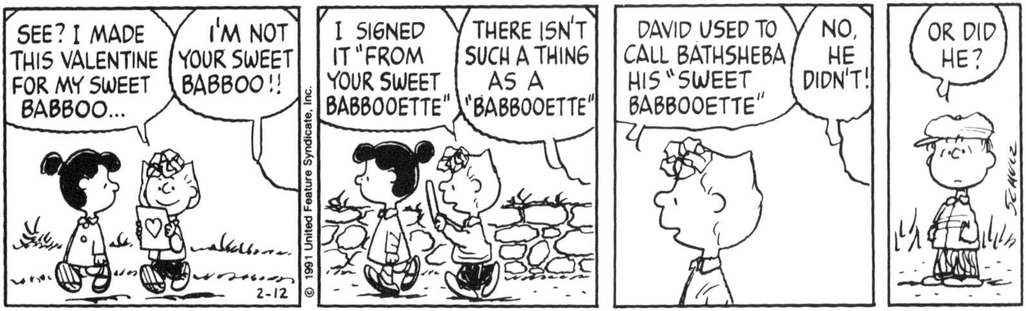
SEE? I MADE THIS VALENTINE FOR MY SWEET BABBOO...
I'M NOT YOUR SWEET BABBOO!!
2-12
© 1991 United Feature Syndicate, Inc.
I SIGNED IT "FROM YOUR SWEET BABBOOETTE"
THERE ISN'T SUCH A THING AS A "BABBOOETTE"
DAVID USED TO CALL BATHSHEBA HIS "SWEET BABBOOETTE"
NO, HE DIDN'T!
OR DID HE?
SCHULZ

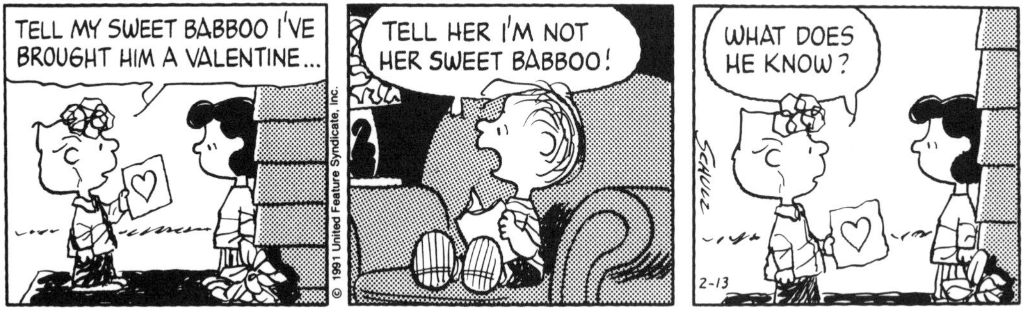
TELL MY SWEET BABBOO I'VE BROUGHT HIM A VALENTINE...
© 1991 United Feature Syndicate, Inc.
TELL HER I'M NOT HER SWEET BABBOO!
WHAT DOES HE KNOW?
SCHULZ
2-13

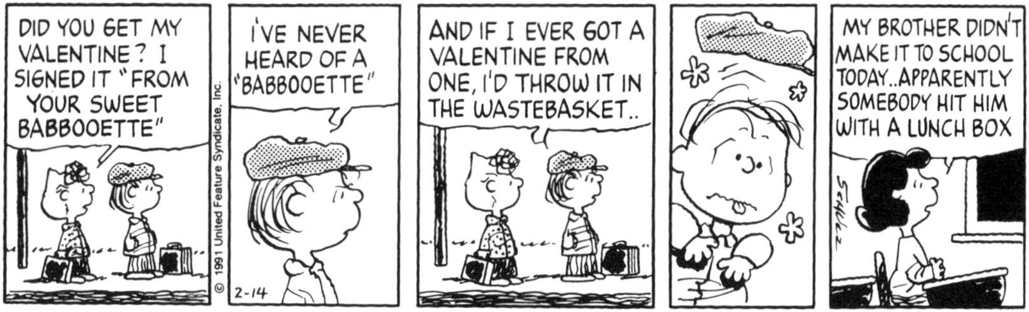
DID YOU GET MY VALENTINE? I SIGNED IT "FROM YOUR SWEET BABBOOETTE"
© 1991 United Feature Syndicate, Inc.
I'VE NEVER HEARD OF A "BABBOOETTE"
2-14
AND IF I EVER GOT A VALENTINE FROM ONE, I'D THROW IT IN THE WASTEBASKET..
MY BROTHER DIDN'T MAKE IT TO SCHOOL TODAY..APPARENTLY SOMEBODY HIT HIM WITH A LUNCH BOX
SCHULZ

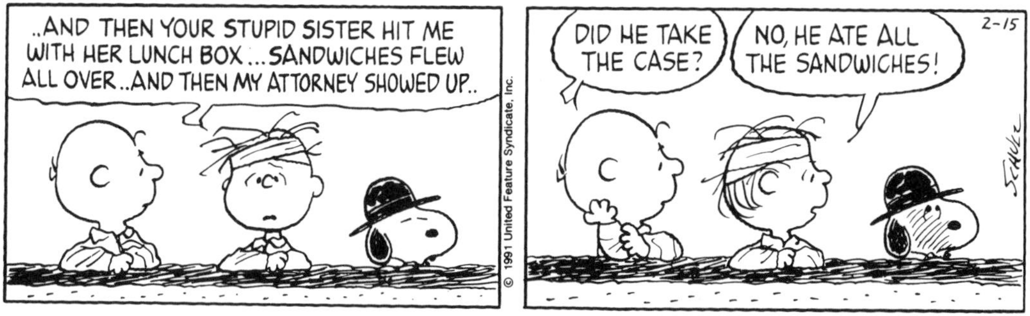
..AND THEN YOUR STUPID SISTER HIT ME WITH HER LUNCH BOX...SANDWICHES FLEW ALL OVER..AND THEN MY ATTORNEY SHOWED UP..
© 1991 United Feature Syndicate, Inc.
2-15
DID HE TAKE THE CASE?
NO, HE ATE ALL THE SANDWICHES!
SCHULZ

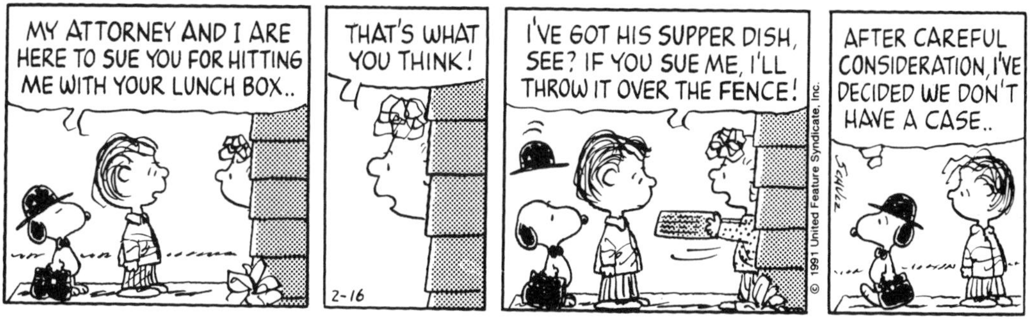
MY ATTORNEY AND I ARE HERE TO SUE YOU FOR HITTING ME WITH YOUR LUNCH BOX..
THAT'S WHAT YOU THINK!
2-16
I'VE GOT HIS SUPPER DISH, SEE? IF YOU SUE ME, I'LL THROW IT OVER THE FENCE!
© 1991 United Feature Syndicate, Inc.
AFTER CAREFUL CONSIDERATION, I'VE DECIDED WE DON'T HAVE A CASE..
SCHULZ

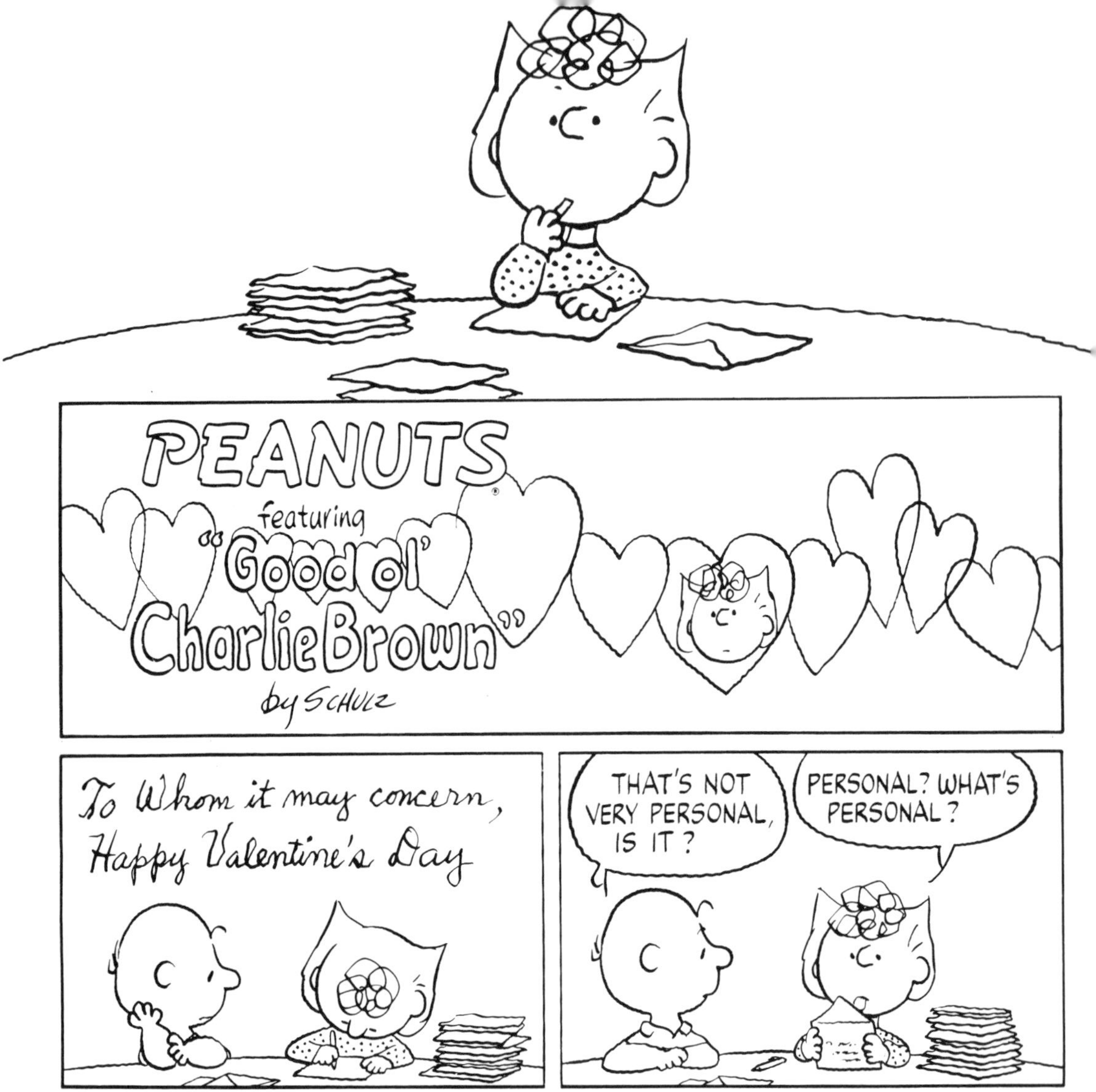
PEANUTS
featuring
"Good ol' Charlie Brown"
by SCHULZ
To Whom it may concern,
Happy Valentine's Day
THAT'S NOT VERY PERSONAL, IS IT?
PERSONAL? WHAT'S PERSONAL?

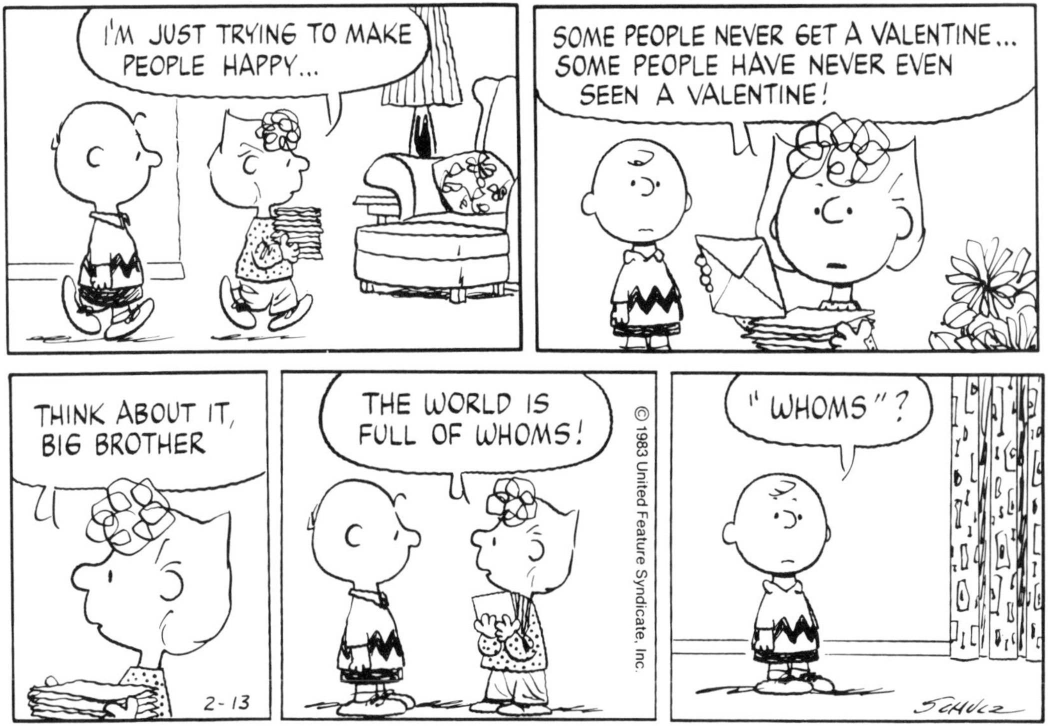
I'M JUST TRYING TO MAKE PEOPLE HAPPY...
SOME PEOPLE NEVER GET A VALENTINE... SOME PEOPLE HAVE NEVER EVEN SEEN A VALENTINE!
THINK ABOUT IT, BIG BROTHER
2-13
THE WORLD IS FULL OF WHOMS!
© 1983 United Feature Syndicate, Inc.
"WHOMS"?
SCHULZ

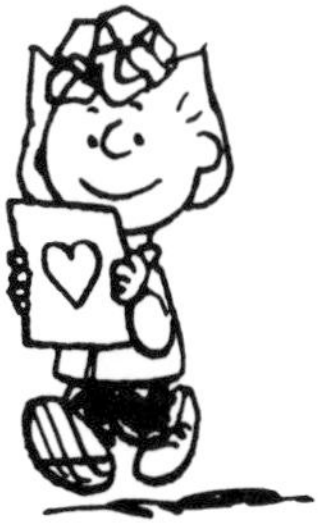

Dear

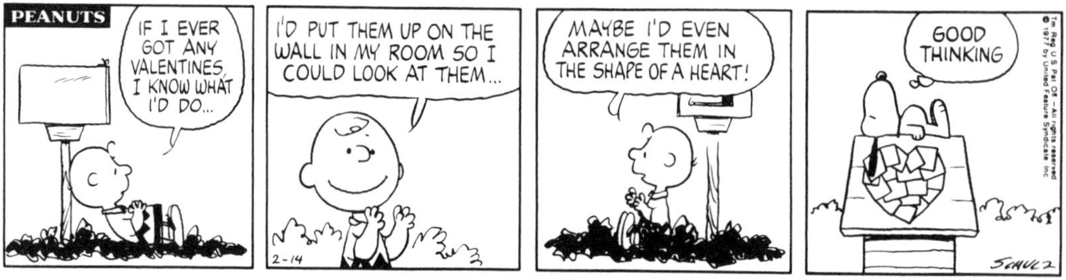
PEANUTS
IF I EVER GOT ANY VALENTINES, I KNOW WHAT I'D DO...
I'D PUT THEM UP ON THE WALL IN MY ROOM SO I COULD LOOK AT THEM...
2-14
MAYBE I'D EVEN ARRANGE THEM IN THE SHAPE OF A HEART!
GOOD THINKING
Tm Reg U S Pat Off —All rights reserved © 1977 by United Feature Syndicate Inc
SCHULZ

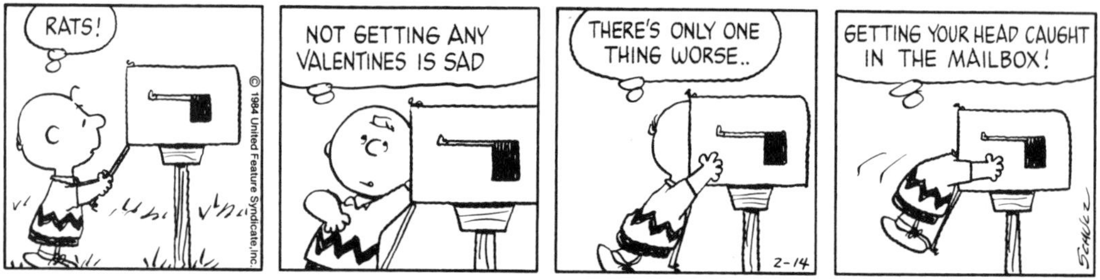
RATS!
© 1984 United Feature Syndicate,Inc.
NOT GETTING ANY VALENTINES IS SAD
THERE'S ONLY ONE THING WORSE..
2-14
GETTING YOUR HEAD CAUGHT IN THE MAILBOX!
SCHULZ

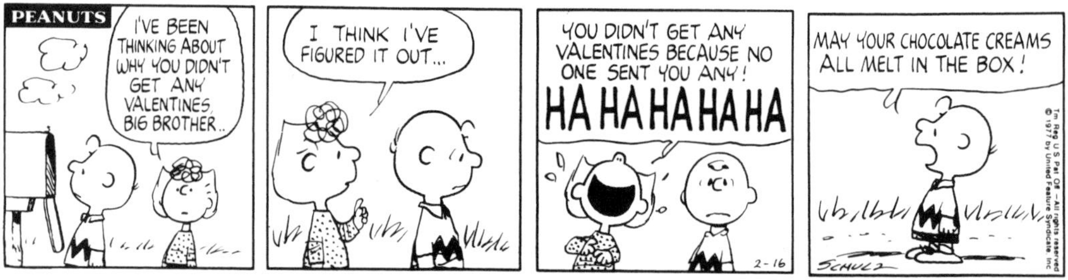
PEANUTS
I'VE BEEN THINKING ABOUT WHY YOU DIDN'T GET ANY VALENTINES, BIG BROTHER..
I THINK I'VE FIGURED IT OUT...
YOU DIDN'T GET ANY VALENTINES BECAUSE NO ONE SENT YOU ANY!
HA HA HA HA HA HA
2-16
MAY YOUR CHOCOLATE CREAMS ALL MELT IN THE BOX!
Tm Reg U S Pat Off —All rights reserved © 1977 by United Feature Syndicate Inc
SCHULZ

Dear Valentine

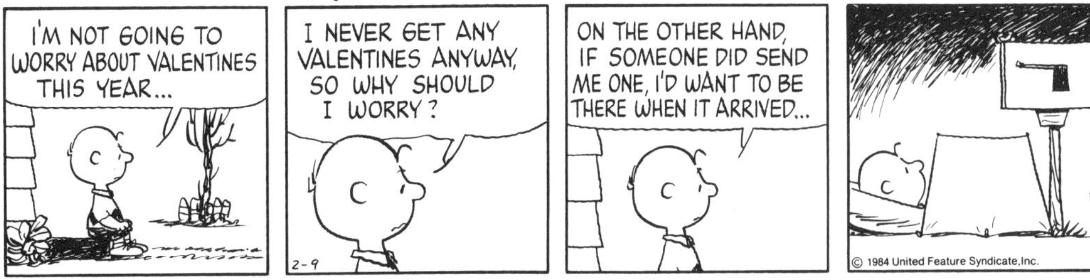
I'M NOT GOING TO WORRY ABOUT VALENTINES THIS YEAR...
I NEVER GET ANY VALENTINES ANYWAY, SO WHY SHOULD I WORRY?
2-9
ON THE OTHER HAND, IF SOMEONE DID SEND ME ONE, I'D WANT TO BE THERE WHEN IT ARRIVED...
SCHULZ
© 1984 United Feature Syndicate, Inc.

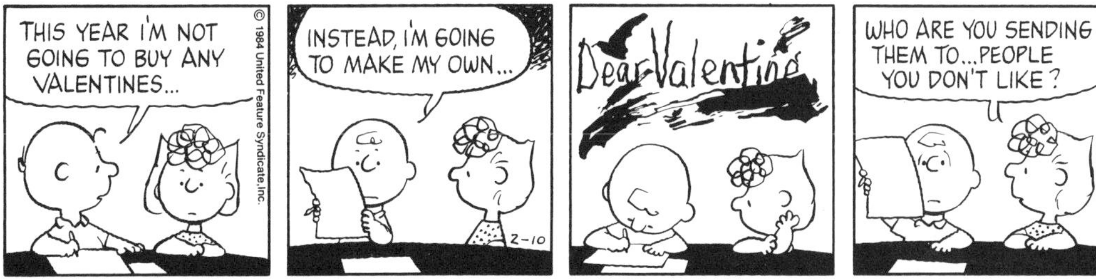
THIS YEAR I'M NOT GOING TO BUY ANY VALENTINES...
© 1984 United Feature Syndicate, Inc.
INSTEAD, I'M GOING TO MAKE MY OWN...
2-10
Dear Valentine
WHO ARE YOU SENDING THEM TO...PEOPLE YOU DON'T LIKE?
SCHULZ

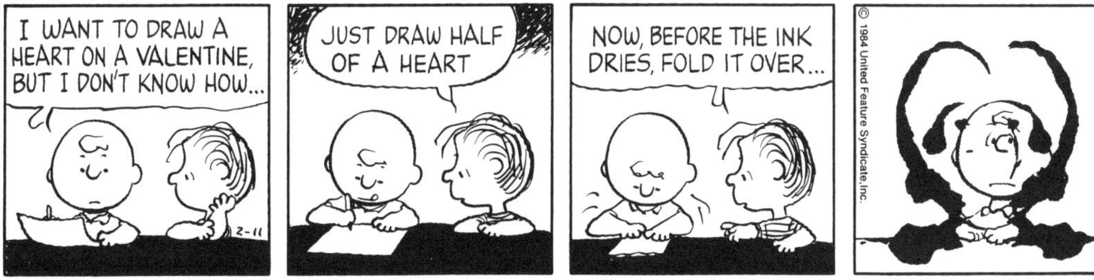
I WANT TO DRAW A HEART ON A VALENTINE, BUT I DON'T KNOW HOW...
2-11
JUST DRAW HALF OF A HEART
NOW, BEFORE THE INK DRIES, FOLD IT OVER...
© 1984 United Feature Syndicate, Inc.
SCHULZ

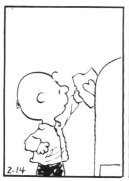

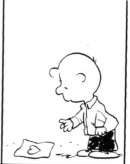

2-14
KEEP YOUR VALENTINE, KID!
IF SHE DOESN'T LOVE YOU ALREADY, A VALENTINE WON'T HELP!
© 1993 United Feature Syndicate, Inc.
I'VE BEEN AROUND A LONG TIME, KID.. I KNOW HOW THESE THINGS GO...
TAKE IT FROM ME, KID..THEY'LL BREAK YOUR HEART...KEEP YOUR VALENTINE!
OH, WELL.. WHAT DO I CARE!?
THAT'S A STRANGE NEW MAILBOX DOWN ON THE CORNER..
SCHULZ

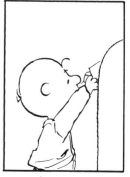

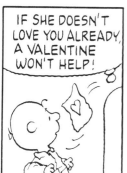

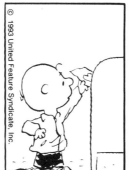

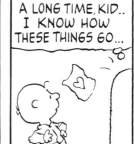

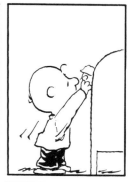

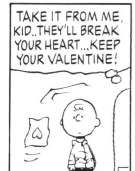

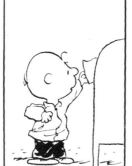

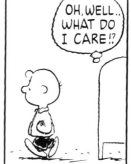

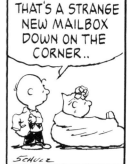

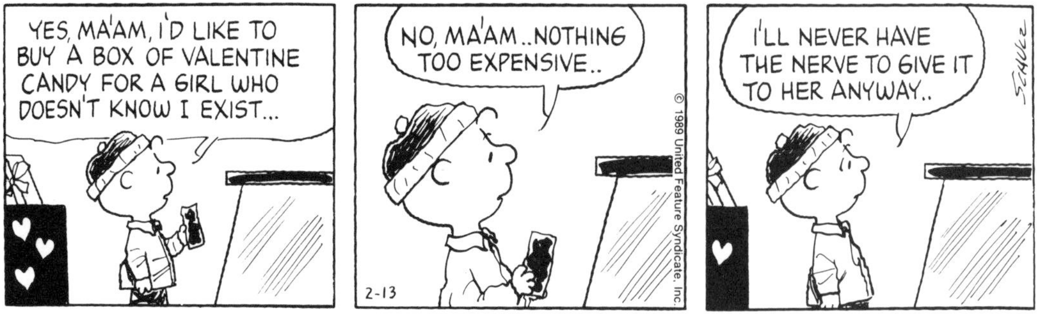
YES, MA'AM, I'D LIKE TO BUY A BOX OF VALENTINE CANDY FOR A GIRL WHO DOESN'T KNOW I EXIST...
NO, MA'AM ..NOTHING TOO EXPENSIVE..
2-13
© 1989 United Feature Syndicate, Inc.
I'LL NEVER HAVE THE NERVE TO GIVE IT TO HER ANYWAY..
SCHULZ

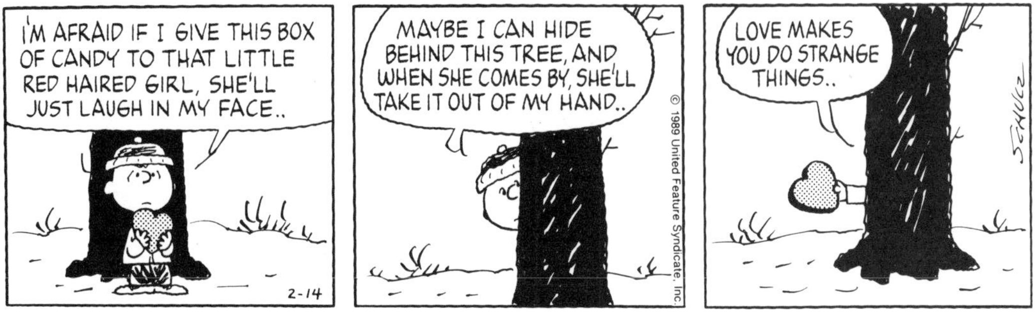
I'M AFRAID IF I GIVE THIS BOX OF CANDY TO THAT LITTLE RED HAIRED GIRL, SHE'LL JUST LAUGH IN MY FACE..
2-14
MAYBE I CAN HIDE BEHIND THIS TREE, AND WHEN SHE COMES BY, SHE'LL TAKE IT OUT OF MY HAND..
© 1989 United Feature Syndicate, Inc.
LOVE MAKES YOU DO STRANGE THINGS..
SCHULZ

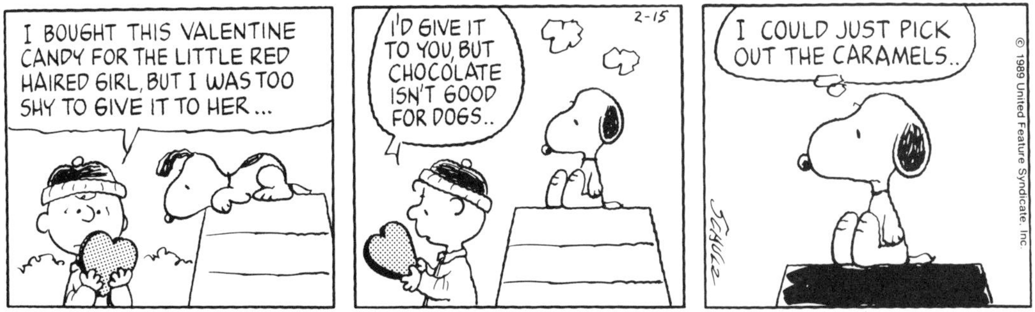
I BOUGHT THIS VALENTINE CANDY FOR THE LITTLE RED HAIRED GIRL, BUT I WAS TOO SHY TO GIVE IT TO HER...
I'D GIVE IT TO YOU, BUT CHOCOLATE ISN'T GOOD FOR DOGS..
2-15
I COULD JUST PICK OUT THE CARAMELS..
SCHULZ
© 1989 United Feature Syndicate, Inc.

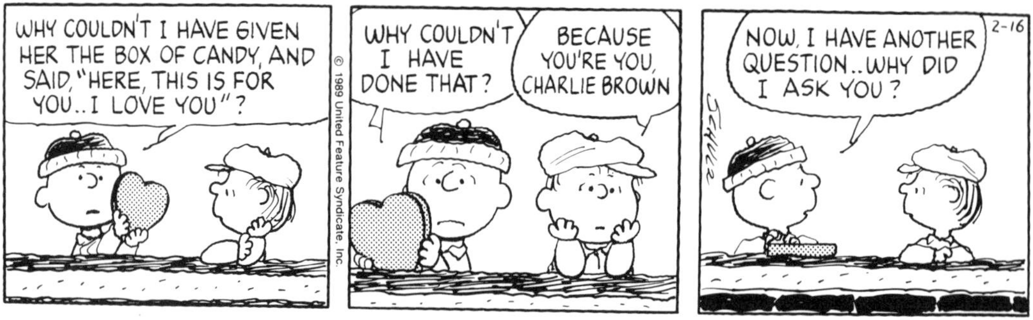
WHY COULDN'T I HAVE GIVEN HER THE BOX OF CANDY, AND SAID, "HERE, THIS IS FOR YOU.. I LOVE YOU"?
© 1989 United Feature Syndicate, Inc.
WHY COULDN'T I HAVE DONE THAT?
BECAUSE YOU'RE YOU, CHARLIE BROWN
2-16
NOW, I HAVE ANOTHER QUESTION.. WHY DID I ASK YOU?

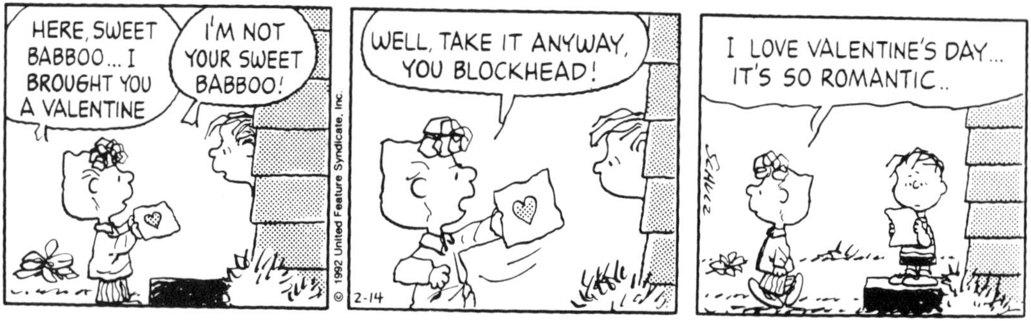
HERE, SWEET BABBOO... I BROUGHT YOU A VALENTINE
I'M NOT YOUR SWEET BABBOO!
© 1992 United Feature Syndicate, Inc.
WELL, TAKE IT ANYWAY, YOU BLOCKHEAD!
2-14
I LOVE VALENTINE'S DAY... IT'S SO ROMANTIC..

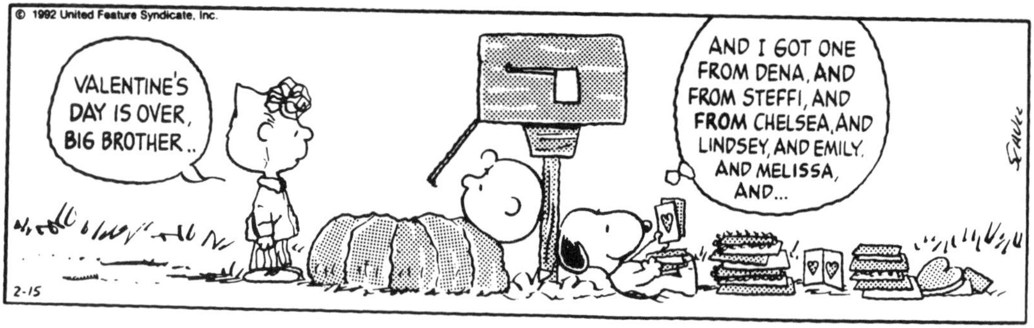
© 1992 United Feature Syndicate, Inc.
VALENTINE'S DAY IS OVER, BIG BROTHER..
AND I GOT ONE FROM DENA, AND FROM STEFFI, AND FROM CHELSEA, AND LINDSEY, AND EMILY, AND MELISSA, AND...
2-15

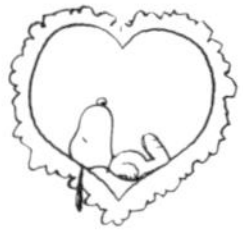

THE COURSE OF TRUE LOVE NEVER DID RUN SMOOTH

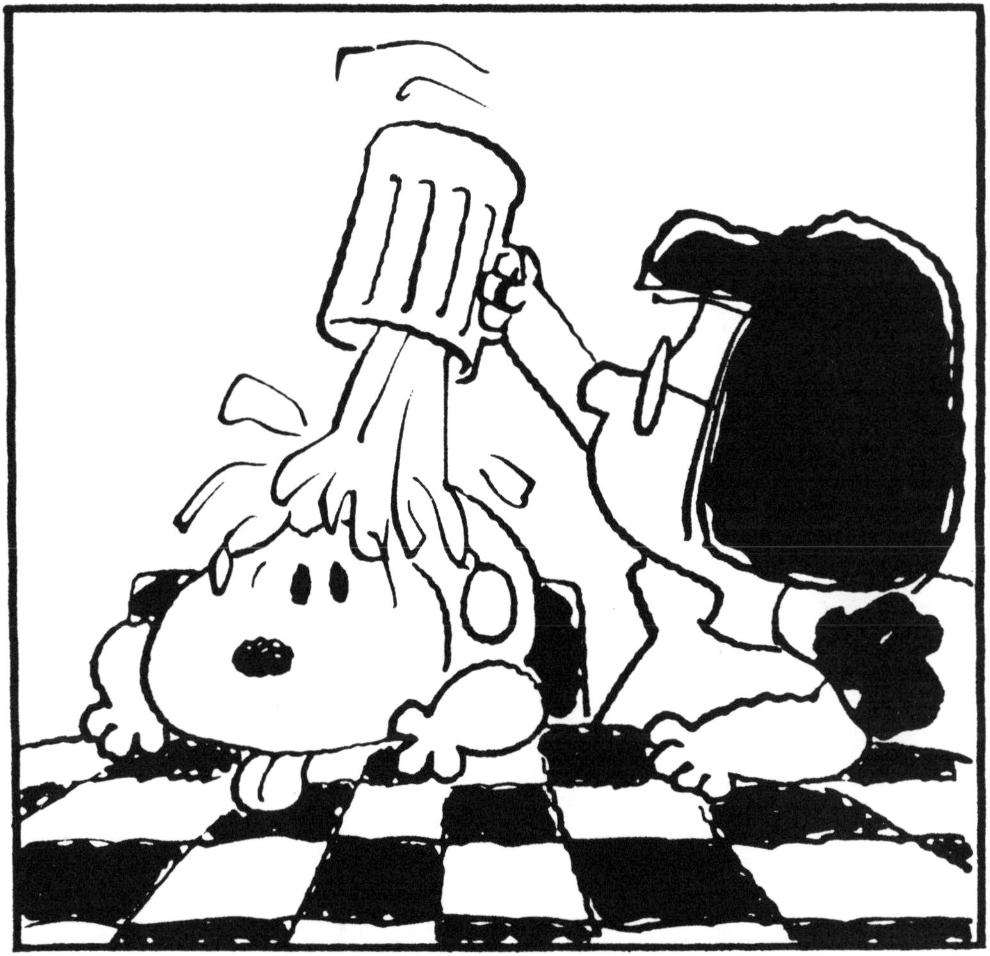

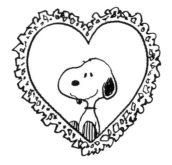

For years, I wanted to draw a tender bittersweet story about Charlie Brown and the little red-haired girl where I would actually show her, but I don't think it will happen. She will probably always remain an off-stage character, for no matter how often I try, I simply can't draw her.

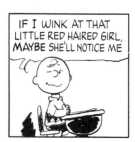

IF I WINK AT THAT LITTLE RED HAIRED GIRL, MAYBE SHE'LL NOTICE ME
1-13
© 1987 United Feature Syndicate, Inc.
I'M NOT GETTING ANY DISTANCE..

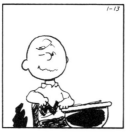

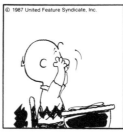

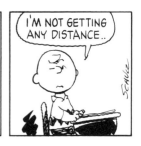

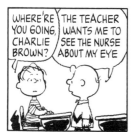

WHERE'RE YOU GOING, CHARLIE BROWN?
THE TEACHER WANTS ME TO SEE THE NURSE ABOUT MY EYE
SHE SAW ME WINKING AT THE LITTLE RED HAIRED GIRL.. SHE THINKS SOMETHING'S WRONG WITH MY EYE...
WHAT AM I GOING TO TELL THE NURSE?
© 1987 United Feature Syndicate, Inc.
1-14
I NEVER KNEW LOVE COULD BE SO MUCH TROUBLE..

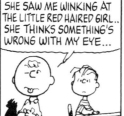

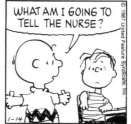

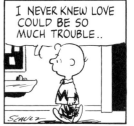

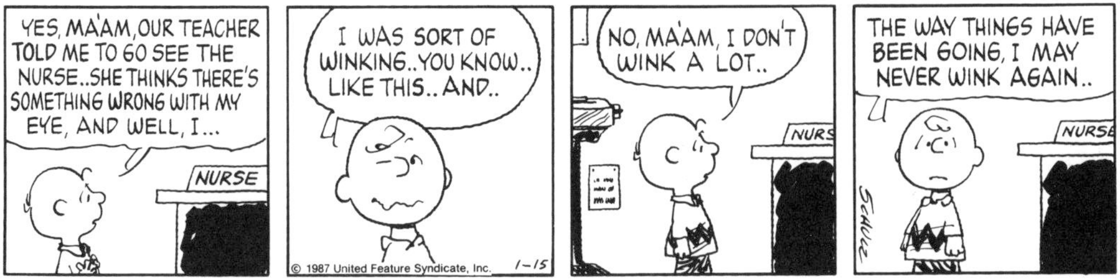
YES, MA'AM, OUR TEACHER TOLD ME TO GO SEE THE NURSE..SHE THINKS THERE'S SOMETHING WRONG WITH MY EYE, AND WELL, I...
NURSE
I WAS SORT OF WINKING..YOU KNOW.. LIKE THIS.. AND..
© 1987 United Feature Syndicate, Inc.
1-15
NO, MA'AM, I DON'T WINK A LOT..
NURS
THE WAY THINGS HAVE BEEN GOING, I MAY NEVER WINK AGAIN..
NURSE
SCHULZ

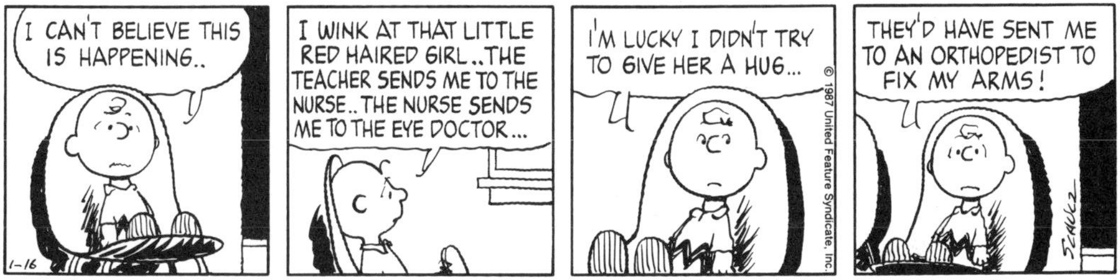
I CAN'T BELIEVE THIS IS HAPPENING..
1-16
I WINK AT THAT LITTLE RED HAIRED GIRL..THE TEACHER SENDS ME TO THE NURSE..THE NURSE SENDS ME TO THE EYE DOCTOR...
I'M LUCKY I DIDN'T TRY TO GIVE HER A HUG...
© 1987 United Feature Syndicate, Inc.
THEY'D HAVE SENT ME TO AN ORTHOPEDIST TO FIX MY ARMS!
SCHULZ

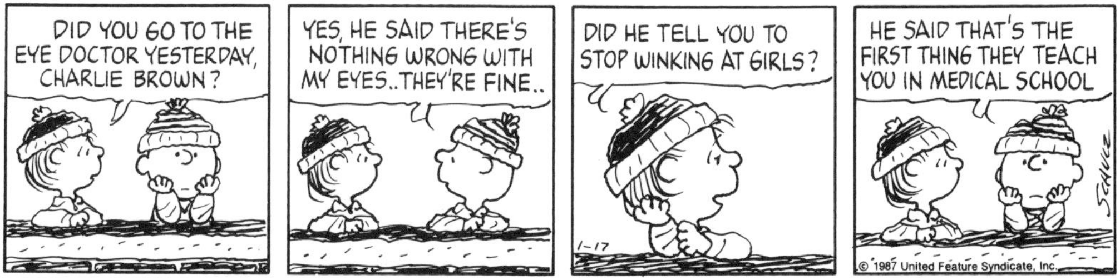
DID YOU GO TO THE EYE DOCTOR YESTERDAY, CHARLIE BROWN?
YES, HE SAID THERE'S NOTHING WRONG WITH MY EYES..THEY'RE FINE..
DID HE TELL YOU TO STOP WINKING AT GIRLS?
1-17
HE SAID THAT'S THE FIRST THING THEY TEACH YOU IN MEDICAL SCHOOL
SCHULZ
© 1987 United Feature Syndicate, Inc.

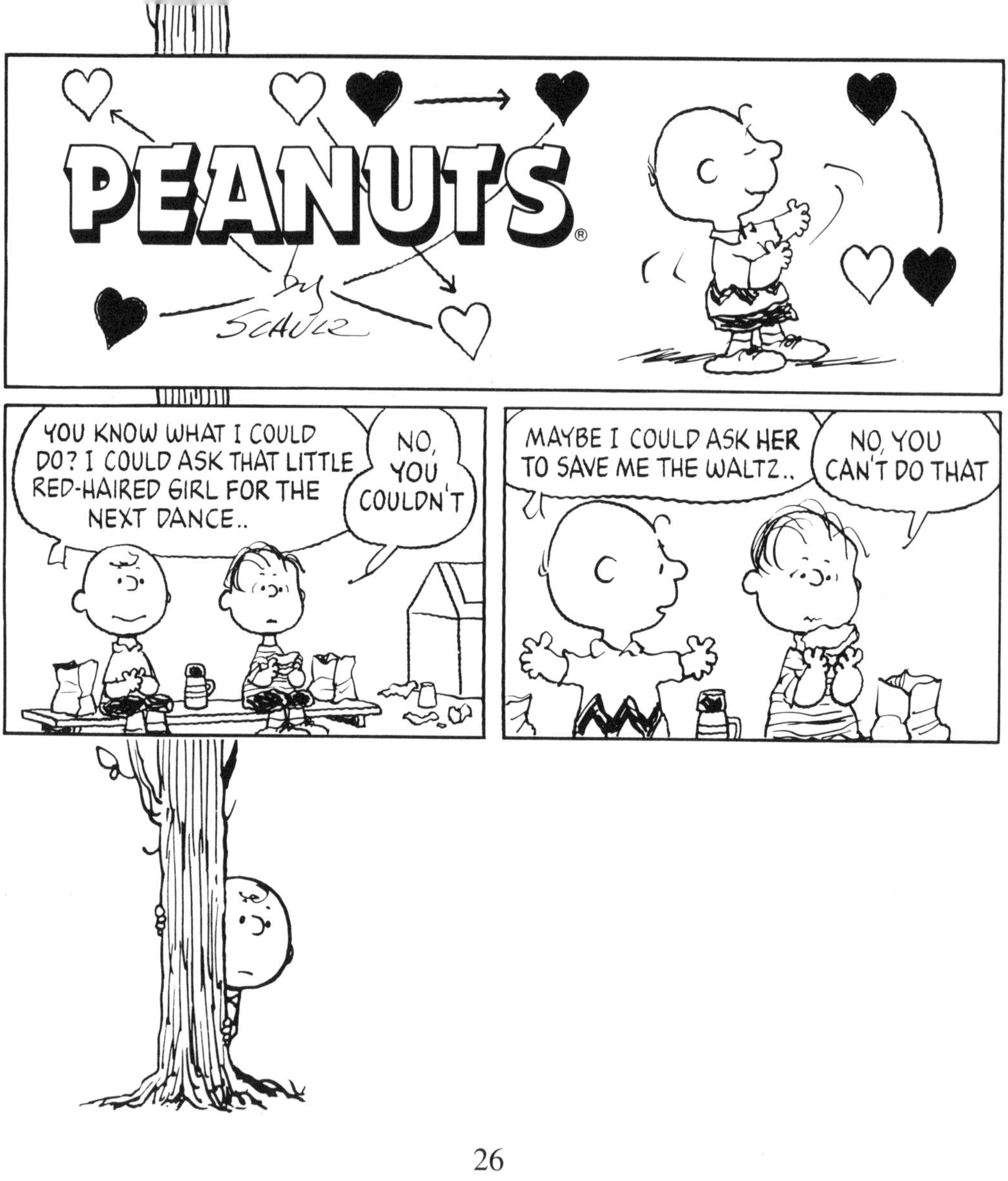
PEANUTS®
YOU KNOW WHAT I COULD DO? I COULD ASK THAT LITTLE RED-HAIRED GIRL FOR THE NEXT DANCE..
NO, YOU COULDN'T
MAYBE I COULD ASK HER TO SAVE ME THE WALTZ..
NO, YOU CAN'T DO THAT

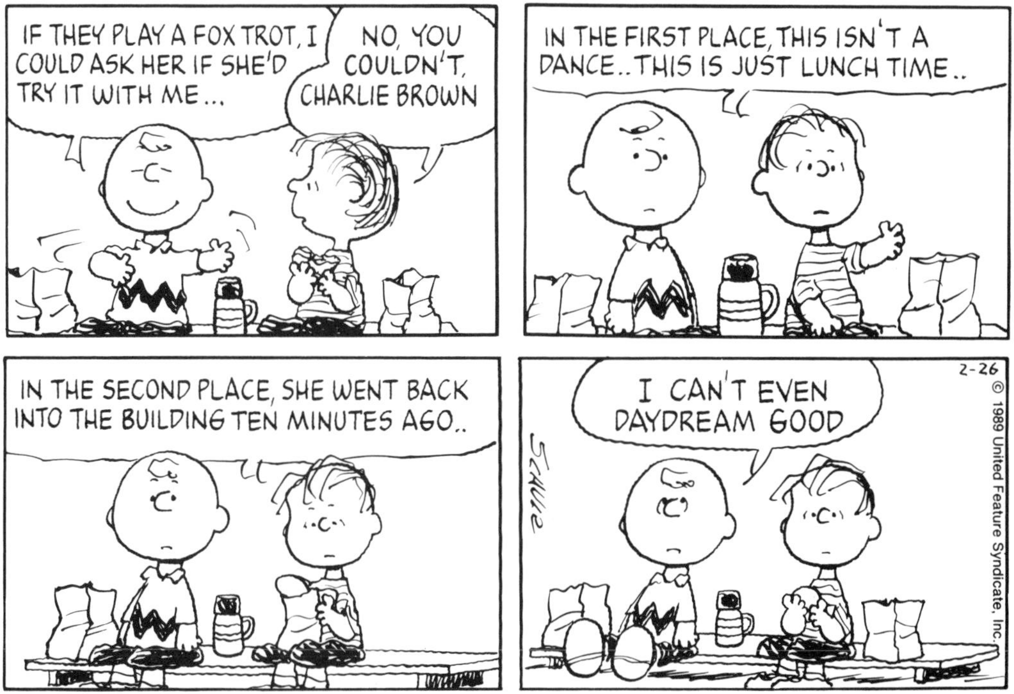
IF THEY PLAY A FOX TROT, I COULD ASK HER IF SHE'D TRY IT WITH ME...
NO, YOU COULDN'T, CHARLIE BROWN
IN THE FIRST PLACE, THIS ISN'T A DANCE.. THIS IS JUST LUNCH TIME..
IN THE SECOND PLACE, SHE WENT BACK INTO THE BUILDING TEN MINUTES AGO..
I CAN'T EVEN DAYDREAM GOOD
2-26
SCHULZ
© 1989 United Feature Syndicate, Inc.

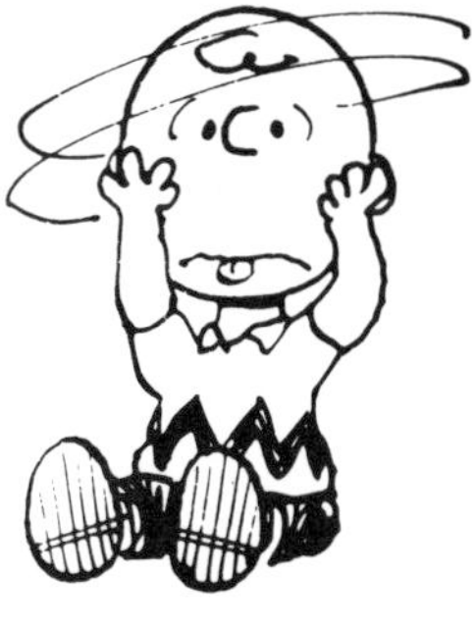

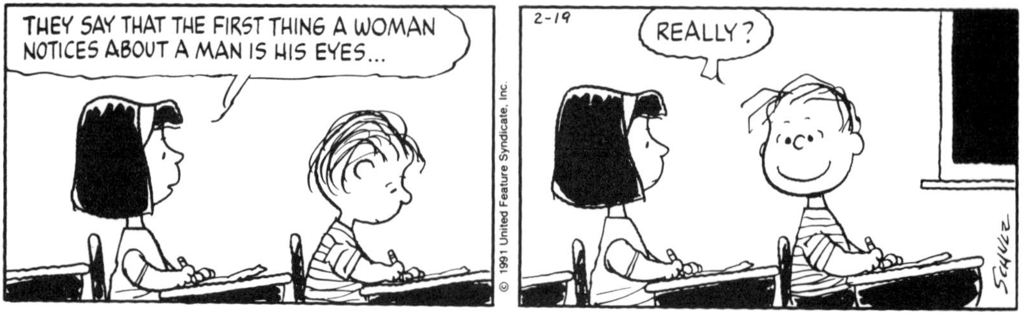
THEY SAY THAT THE FIRST THING A WOMAN NOTICES ABOUT A MAN IS HIS EYES...
© 1991 United Feature Syndicate, Inc.
2-19
REALLY?

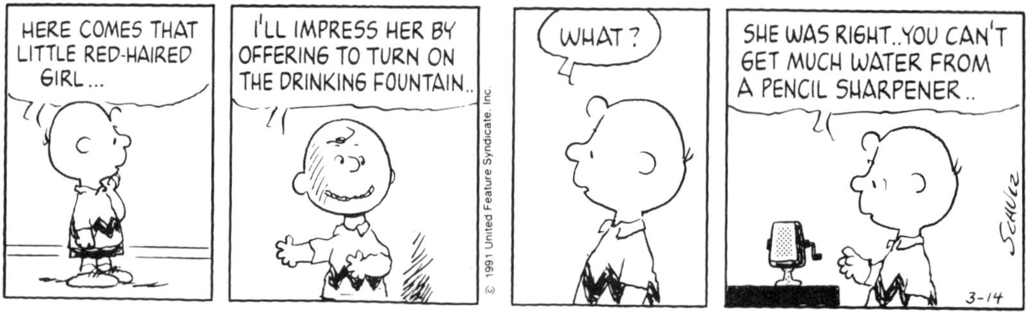
HERE COMES THAT LITTLE RED-HAIRED GIRL...
I'LL IMPRESS HER BY OFFERING TO TURN ON THE DRINKING FOUNTAIN..
© 1991 United Feature Syndicate, Inc.
WHAT?
SHE WAS RIGHT..YOU CAN'T GET MUCH WATER FROM A PENCIL SHARPENER..
3-14

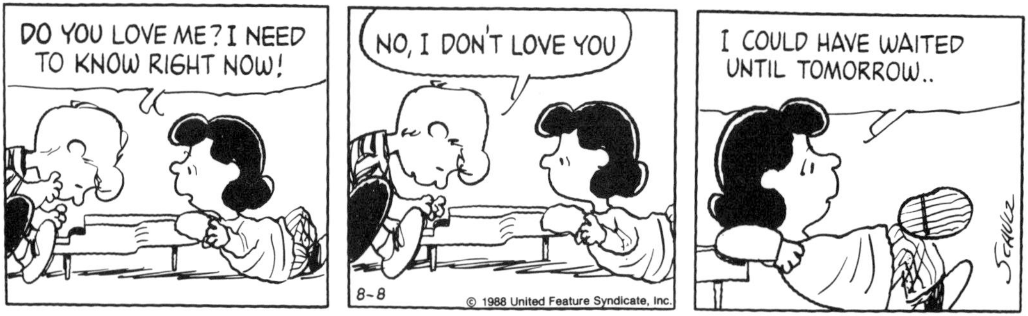
DO YOU LOVE ME? I NEED TO KNOW RIGHT NOW!
NO, I DON'T LOVE YOU
8-8
© 1988 United Feature Syndicate, Inc.
I COULD HAVE WAITED UNTIL TOMORROW..

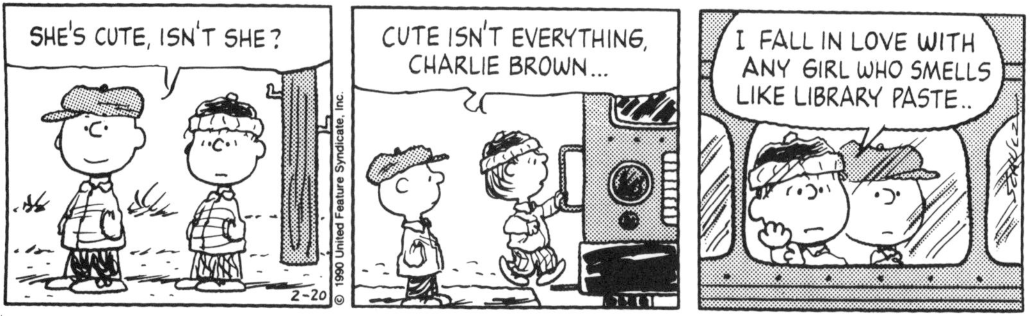
SHE'S CUTE, ISN'T SHE?
2-20
© 1990 United Feature Syndicate, Inc.
CUTE ISN'T EVERYTHING, CHARLIE BROWN...
I FALL IN LOVE WITH ANY GIRL WHO SMELLS LIKE LIBRARY PASTE..
SCHULZ

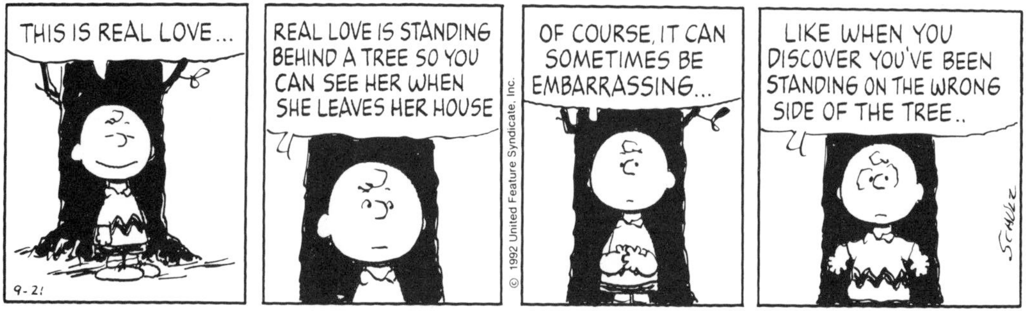
THIS IS REAL LOVE...
9-21
REAL LOVE IS STANDING BEHIND A TREE SO YOU CAN SEE HER WHEN SHE LEAVES HER HOUSE
© 1992 United Feature Syndicate, Inc.
OF COURSE, IT CAN SOMETIMES BE EMBARRASSING...
LIKE WHEN YOU DISCOVER YOU'VE BEEN STANDING ON THE WRONG SIDE OF THE TREE..
SCHULZ

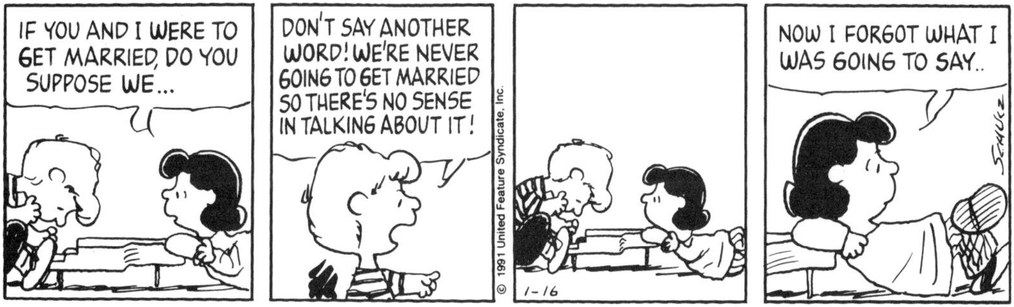
IF YOU AND I WERE TO GET MARRIED, DO YOU SUPPOSE WE...
DON'T SAY ANOTHER WORD! WE'RE NEVER GOING TO GET MARRIED SO THERE'S NO SENSE IN TALKING ABOUT IT!
© 1991 United Feature Syndicate, Inc.
1-16
NOW I FORGOT WHAT I WAS GOING TO SAY..
SCHULZ

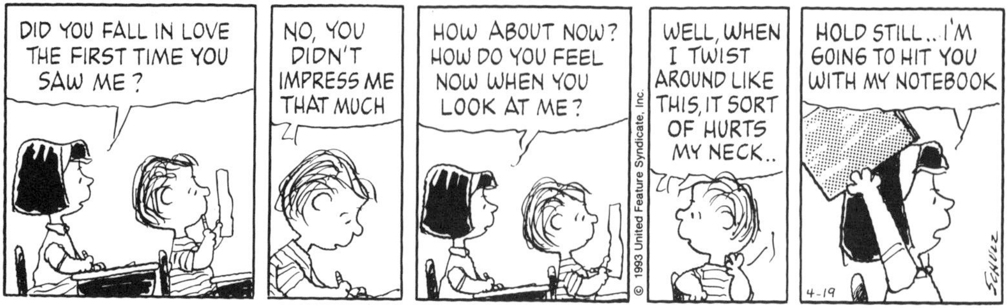
DID YOU FALL IN LOVE THE FIRST TIME YOU SAW ME?
NO, YOU DIDN'T IMPRESS ME THAT MUCH
HOW ABOUT NOW? HOW DO YOU FEEL NOW WHEN YOU LOOK AT ME?
© 1993 United Feature Syndicate, Inc.
WELL, WHEN I TWIST AROUND LIKE THIS, IT SORT OF HURTS MY NECK..
HOLD STILL.. I'M GOING TO HIT YOU WITH MY NOTEBOOK
4-19
SCHULZ

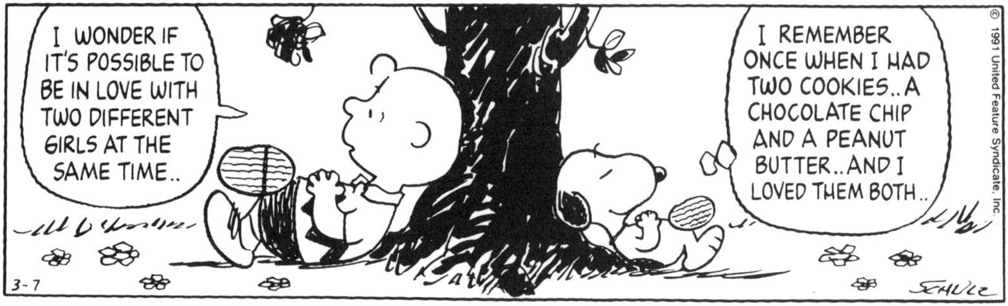
I WONDER IF IT'S POSSIBLE TO BE IN LOVE WITH TWO DIFFERENT GIRLS AT THE SAME TIME..
I REMEMBER ONCE WHEN I HAD TWO COOKIES.. A CHOCOLATE CHIP AND A PEANUT BUTTER.. AND I LOVED THEM BOTH..
© 1991 United Feature Syndicate, Inc.
3-7
SCHULZ

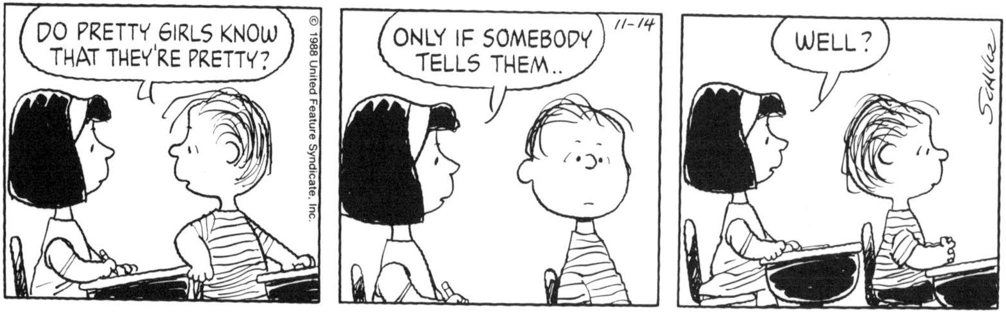
DO PRETTY GIRLS KNOW THAT THEY'RE PRETTY?
© 1988 United Feature Syndicate, Inc.
ONLY IF SOMEBODY TELLS THEM..
11-14
WELL?
SCHULZ

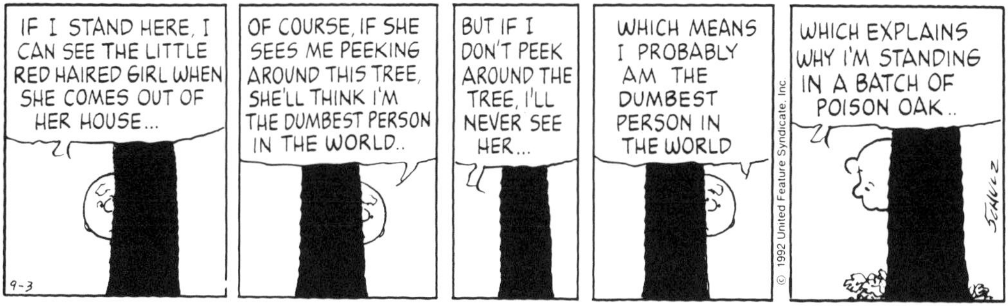
IF I STAND HERE, I CAN SEE THE LITTLE RED HAIRED GIRL WHEN SHE COMES OUT OF HER HOUSE...
OF COURSE, IF SHE SEES ME PEEKING AROUND THIS TREE, SHE'LL THINK I'M THE DUMBEST PERSON IN THE WORLD..
BUT IF I DON'T PEEK AROUND THE TREE, I'LL NEVER SEE HER...
WHICH MEANS I PROBABLY AM THE DUMBEST PERSON IN THE WORLD
WHICH EXPLAINS WHY I'M STANDING IN A BATCH OF POISON OAK..
9-3
© 1992 United Feature Syndicate, Inc.
SCHULZ

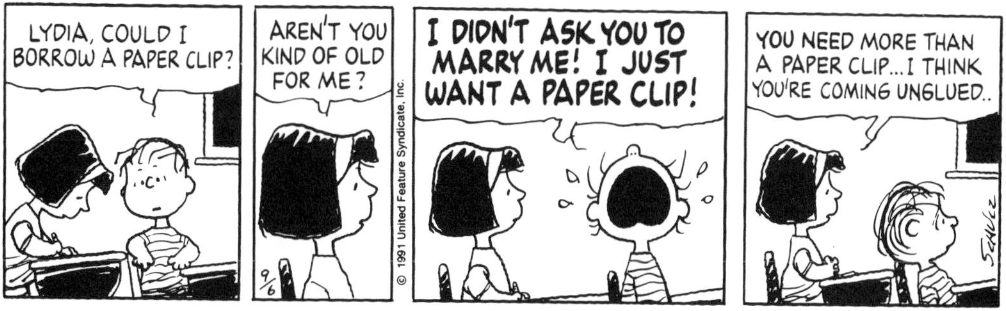
LYDIA, COULD I BORROW A PAPER CLIP?
AREN'T YOU KIND OF OLD FOR ME?
9/6
© 1991 United Feature Syndicate, Inc.
I DIDN'T ASK YOU TO MARRY ME! I JUST WANT A PAPER CLIP!
YOU NEED MORE THAN A PAPER CLIP...I THINK YOU'RE COMING UNGLUED..
SCHULZ

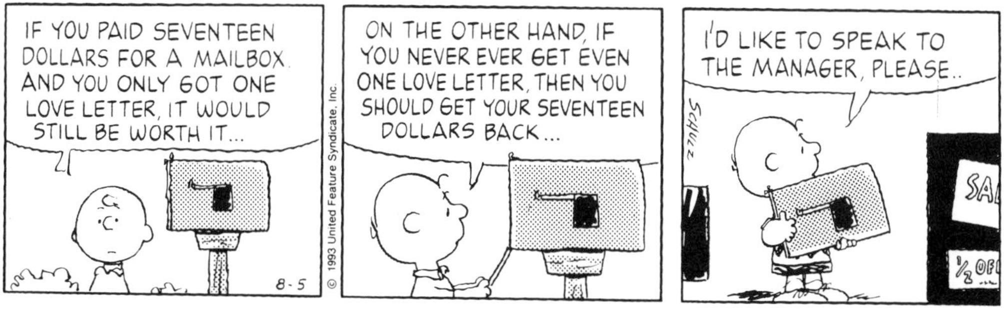
IF YOU PAID SEVENTEEN DOLLARS FOR A MAILBOX AND YOU ONLY GOT ONE LOVE LETTER, IT WOULD STILL BE WORTH IT...
8-5
© 1993 United Feature Syndicate, Inc.
ON THE OTHER HAND, IF YOU NEVER EVER GET EVEN ONE LOVE LETTER, THEN YOU SHOULD GET YOUR SEVENTEEN DOLLARS BACK...
I'D LIKE TO SPEAK TO THE MANAGER, PLEASE..
SCHULZ

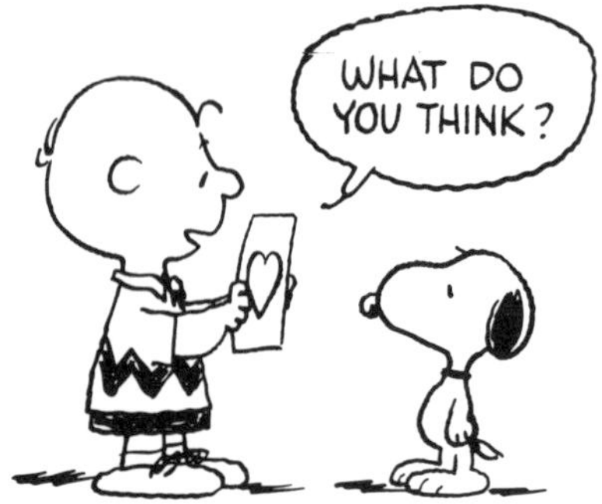
WHAT DO YOU THINK?

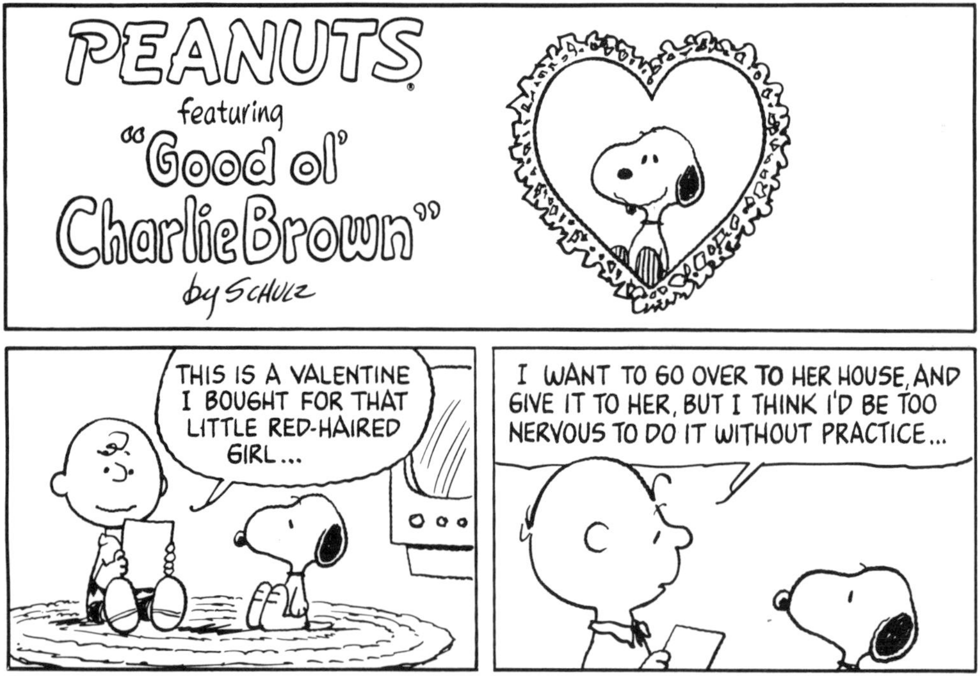
PEANUTS®
featuring
"Good ol' Charlie Brown"
by SCHULZ
THIS IS A VALENTINE I BOUGHT FOR THAT LITTLE RED-HAIRED GIRL...
I WANT TO GO OVER TO HER HOUSE, AND GIVE IT TO HER, BUT I THINK I'D BE TOO NERVOUS TO DO IT WITHOUT PRACTICE...

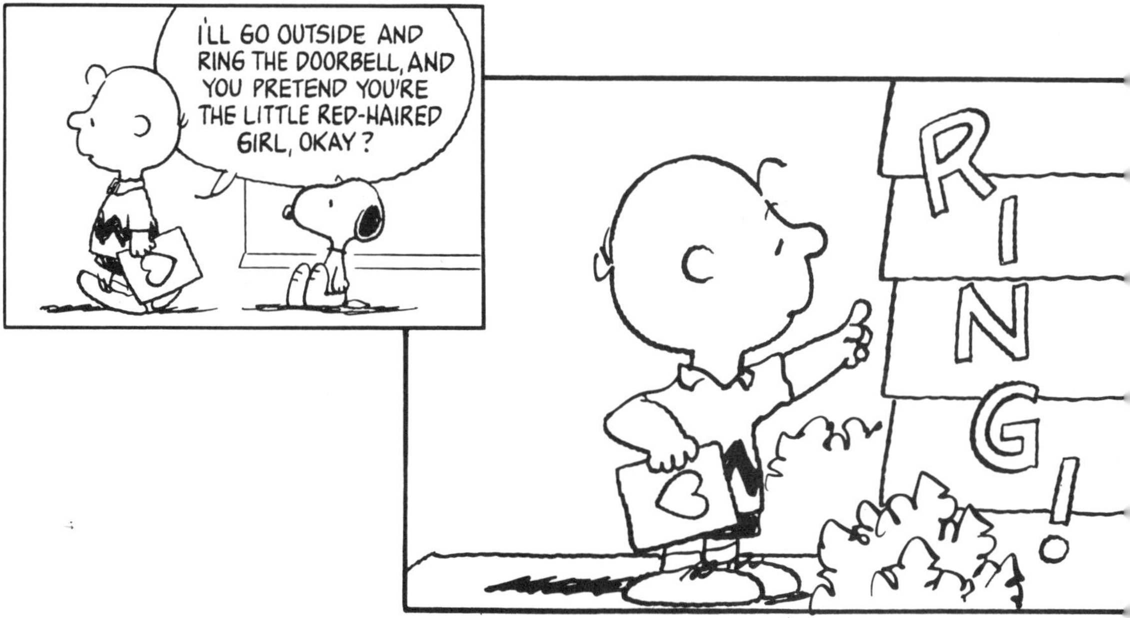
I'LL GO OUTSIDE AND RING THE DOORBELL, AND YOU PRETEND YOU'RE THE LITTLE RED-HAIRED GIRL, OKAY?
RING!

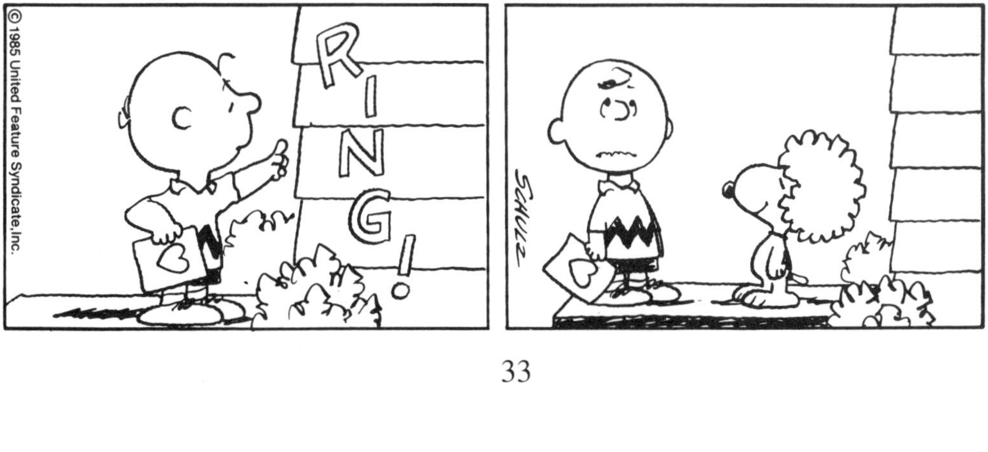
RING!
SCHULZ

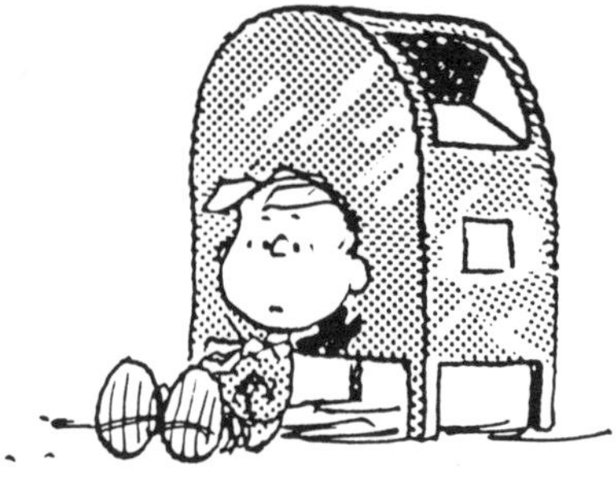

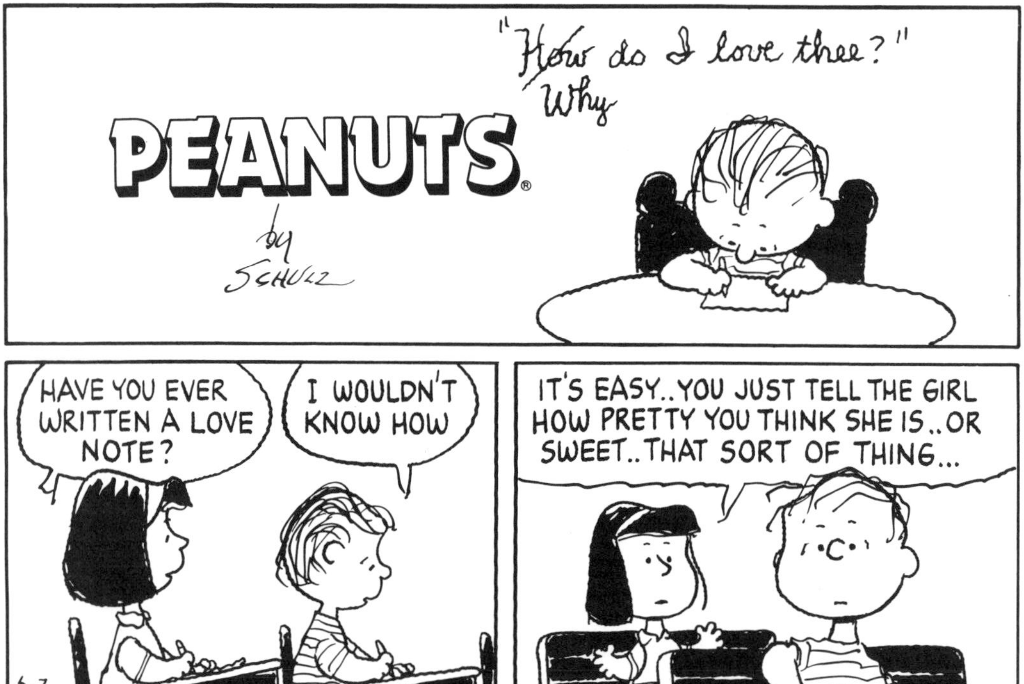
"How do I love thee?"
Why
PEANUTS®
by SCHULZ
HAVE YOU EVER WRITTEN A LOVE NOTE?
I WOULDN'T KNOW HOW
IT'S EASY..YOU JUST TELL THE GIRL HOW PRETTY YOU THINK SHE IS..OR SWEET..THAT SORT OF THING...
6-7

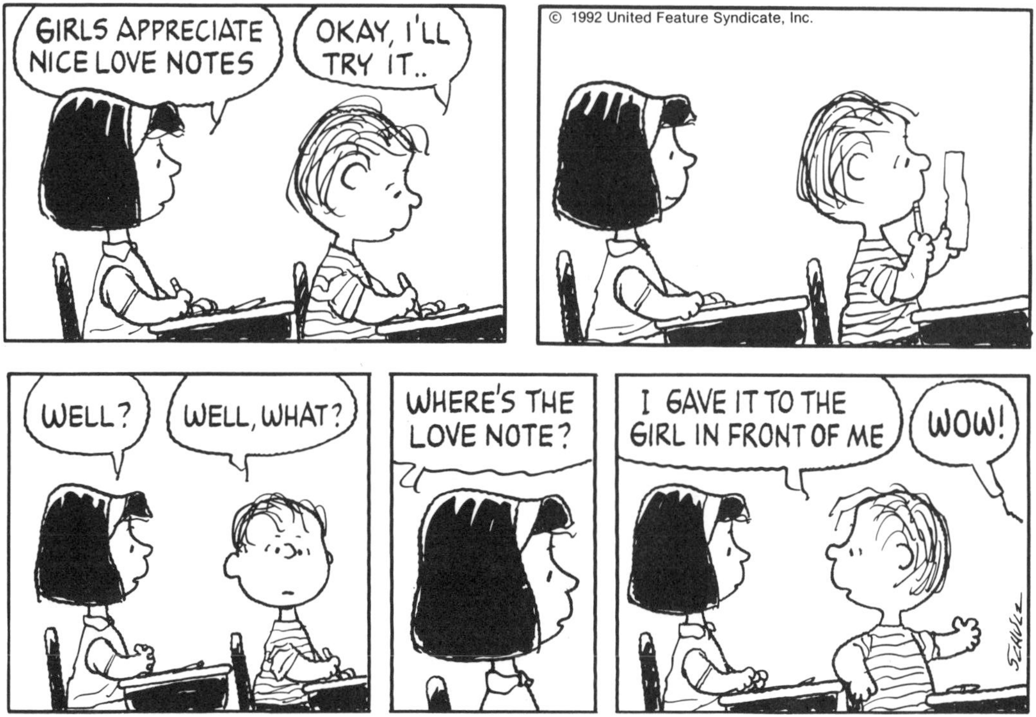
GIRLS APPRECIATE NICE LOVE NOTES
OKAY, I'LL TRY IT..
WELL?
WELL, WHAT?
WHERE'S THE LOVE NOTE?
I GAVE IT TO THE GIRL IN FRONT OF ME
WOW!
SCHULZ

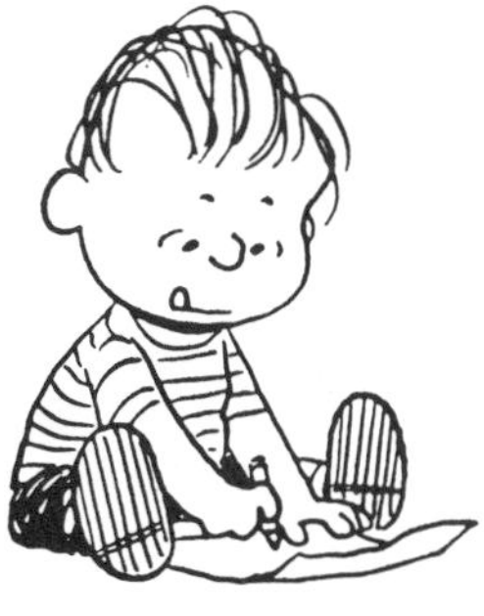

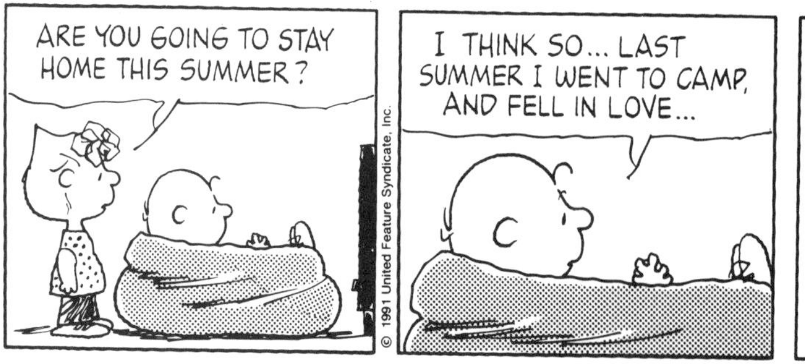
ARE YOU GOING TO STAY HOME THIS SUMMER?
© 1991 United Feature Syndicate, Inc.
I THINK SO... LAST SUMMER I WENT TO CAMP, AND FELL IN LOVE...
..AND THE POOL, AND THE LAKE AND THE POISON OAK!
7-1
SCHULZ

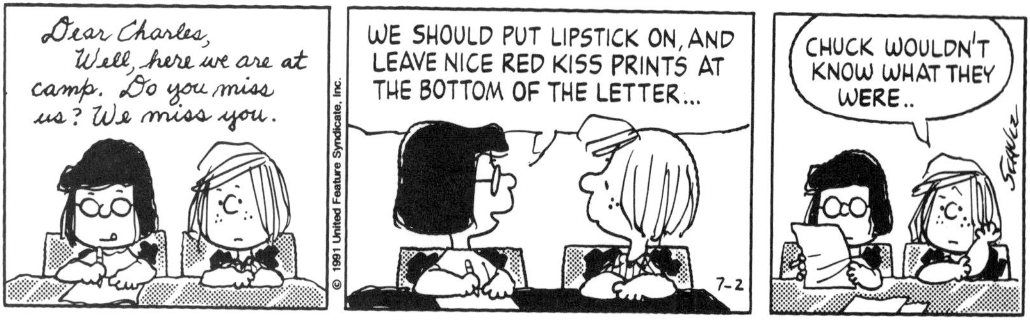
Dear Charles,
Well, here we are at camp. Do you miss us? We miss you.
© 1991 United Feature Syndicate, Inc.
WE SHOULD PUT LIPSTICK ON, AND LEAVE NICE RED KISS PRINTS AT THE BOTTOM OF THE LETTER...
7-2
CHUCK WOULDN'T KNOW WHAT THEY WERE..
SCHULZ

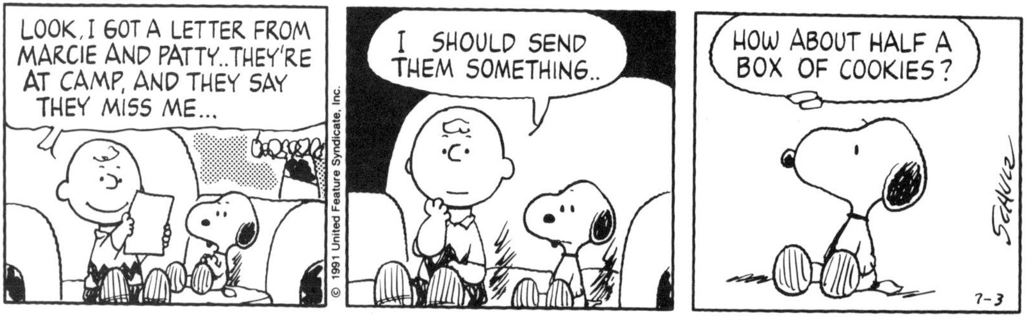
LOOK, I GOT A LETTER FROM MARCIE AND PATTY..THEY'RE AT CAMP, AND THEY SAY THEY MISS ME...
© 1991 United Feature Syndicate, Inc.
I SHOULD SEND THEM SOMETHING..
HOW ABOUT HALF A BOX OF COOKIES?
SCHULZ
7-3

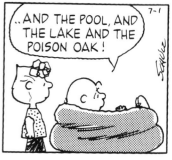

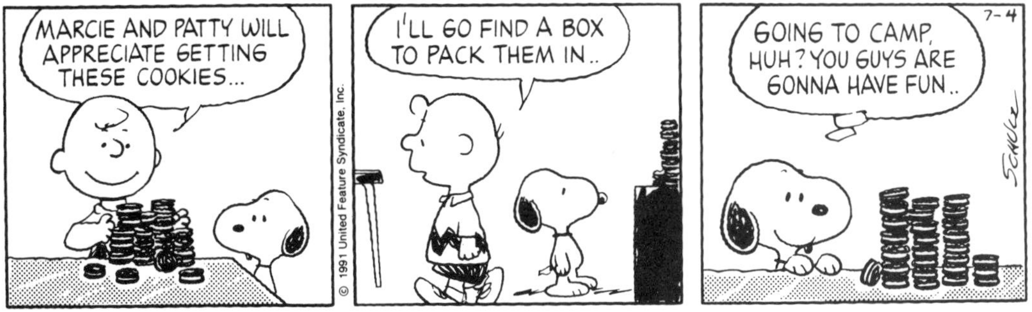
MARCIE AND PATTY WILL APPRECIATE GETTING THESE COOKIES...
© 1991 United Feature Syndicate, Inc.
I'LL GO FIND A BOX TO PACK THEM IN..
7-4
GOING TO CAMP, HUH? YOU GUYS ARE GONNA HAVE FUN..
SCHULZ

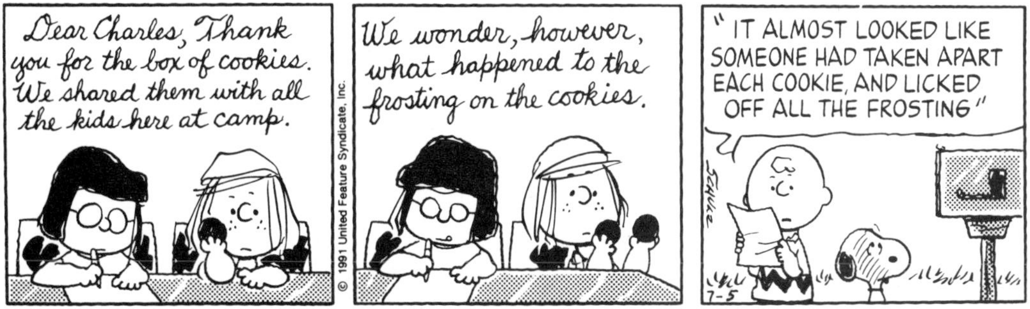
Dear Charles, Thank you for the box of cookies. We shared them with all the kids here at camp.
© 1991 United Feature Syndicate, Inc.
We wonder, however, what happened to the frosting on the cookies.
"IT ALMOST LOOKED LIKE SOMEONE HAD TAKEN APART EACH COOKIE, AND LICKED OFF ALL THE FROSTING"
SCHULZ
7-5

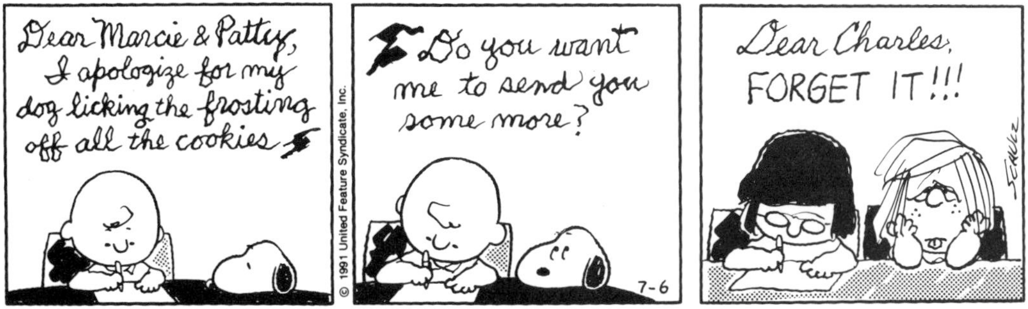
Dear Marcie & Patty, I apologize for my dog licking the frosting off all the cookies
© 1991 United Feature Syndicate, Inc.
Do you want me to send you some more?
7-6
Dear Charles, FORGET IT!!!
SCHULZ

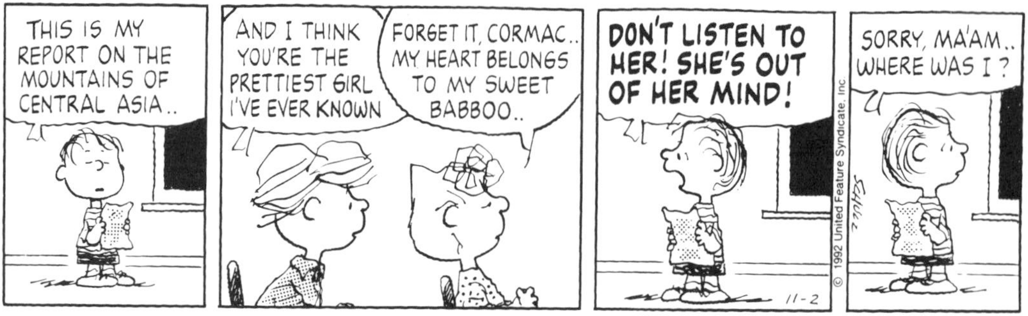
THIS IS MY REPORT ON THE MOUNTAINS OF CENTRAL ASIA..
AND I THINK YOU'RE THE PRETTIEST GIRL I'VE EVER KNOWN
FORGET IT, CORMAC.. MY HEART BELONGS TO MY SWEET BABBOO..
DON'T LISTEN TO HER! SHE'S OUT OF HER MIND!
11-2
© 1992 United Feature Syndicate, Inc.
SORRY, MA'AM.. WHERE WAS I ?

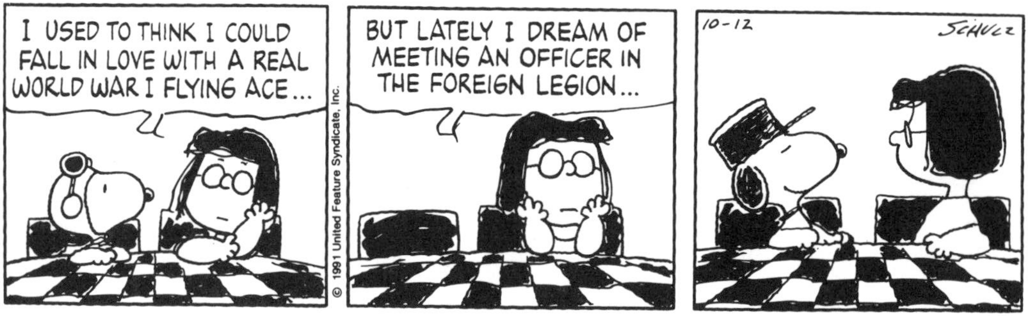
I USED TO THINK I COULD FALL IN LOVE WITH A REAL WORLD WAR I FLYING ACE...
© 1991 United Feature Syndicate, Inc.
BUT LATELY I DREAM OF MEETING AN OFFICER IN THE FOREIGN LEGION...
10-12

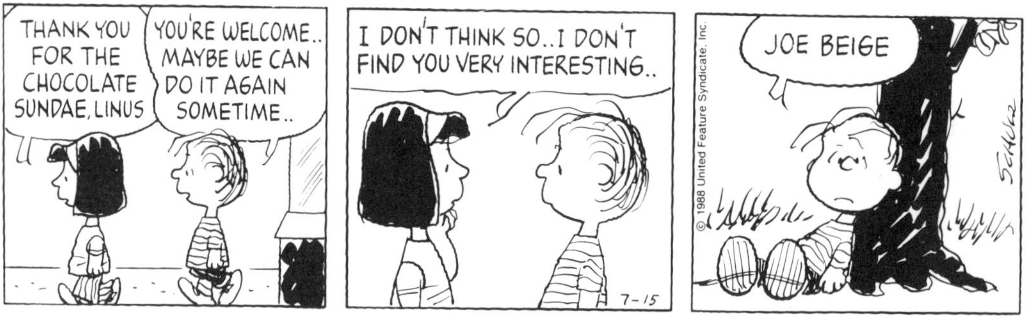
THANK YOU FOR THE CHOCOLATE SUNDAE, LINUS
YOU'RE WELCOME.. MAYBE WE CAN DO IT AGAIN SOMETIME..
I DON'T THINK SO..I DON'T FIND YOU VERY INTERESTING..
7-15
© 1988 United Feature Syndicate, Inc.
JOE BEIGE

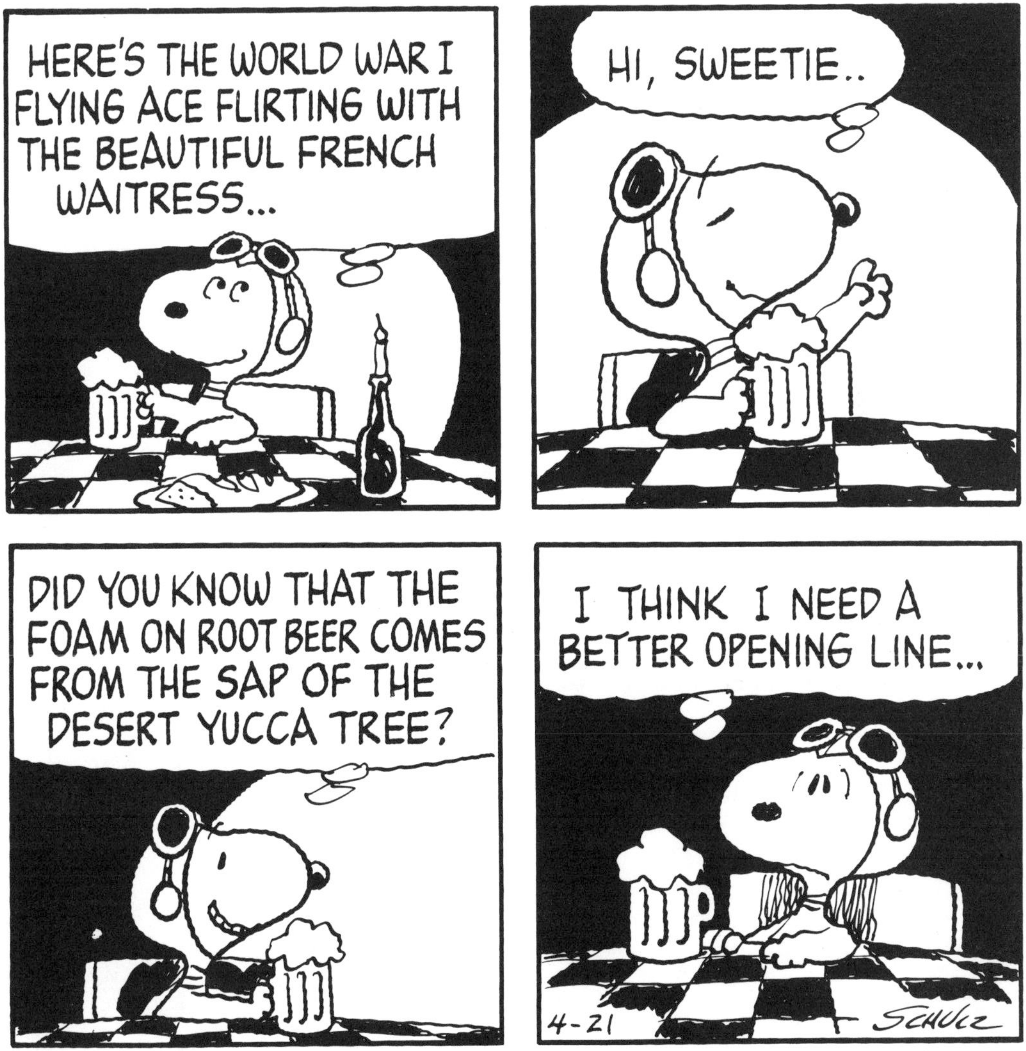
HERE'S THE WORLD WAR I FLYING ACE FLIRTING WITH THE BEAUTIFUL FRENCH WAITRESS...
HI, SWEETIE..
DID YOU KNOW THAT THE FOAM ON ROOT BEER COMES FROM THE SAP OF THE DESERT YUCCA TREE?
I THINK I NEED A BETTER OPENING LINE...
4-21
SCHULZ

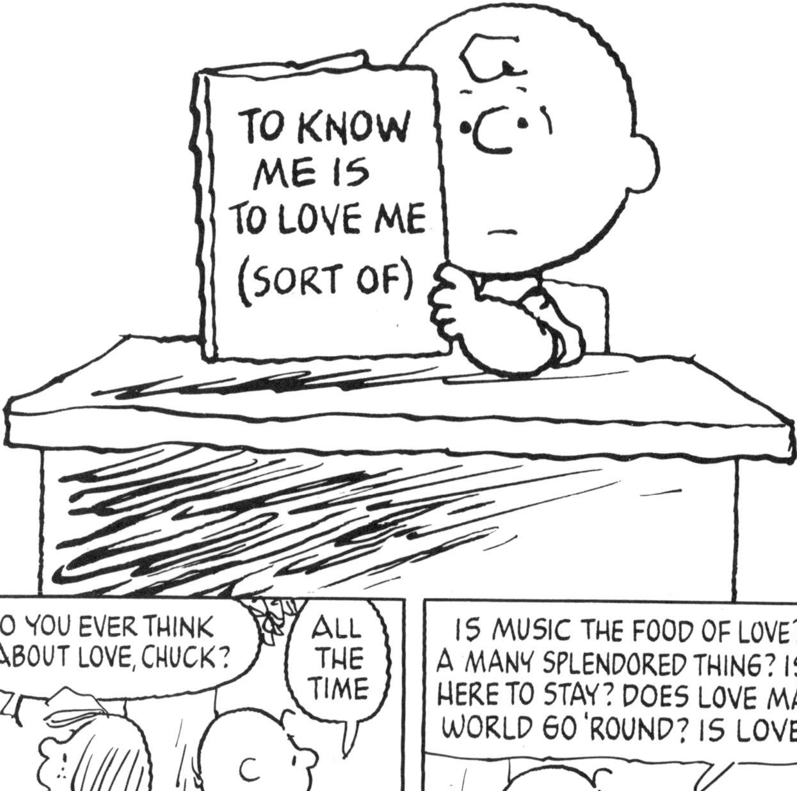
TO KNOW
ME IS
TO LOVE ME
(SORT OF)

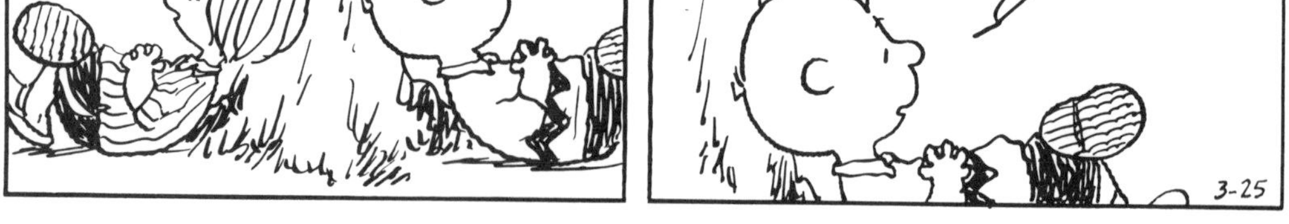
DO YOU EVER THINK ABOUT LOVE, CHUCK?
ALL THE TIME
IS MUSIC THE FOOD OF LOVE? IS LOVE A MANY SPLENDORED THING? IS LOVE HERE TO STAY? DOES LOVE MAKE THE WORLD GO 'ROUND? IS LOVE A...
3-25

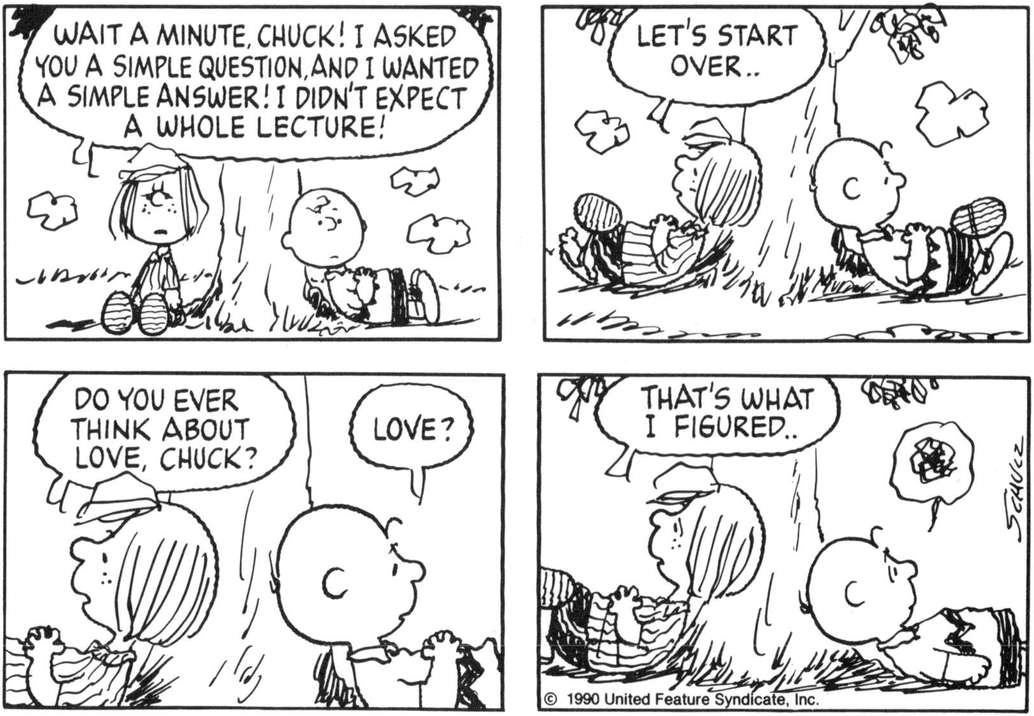
WAIT A MINUTE, CHUCK! I ASKED YOU A SIMPLE QUESTION, AND I WANTED A SIMPLE ANSWER! I DIDN'T EXPECT A WHOLE LECTURE!
LET'S START OVER..
DO YOU EVER THINK ABOUT LOVE, CHUCK?
LOVE?
THAT'S WHAT I FIGURED..
SCHULZ

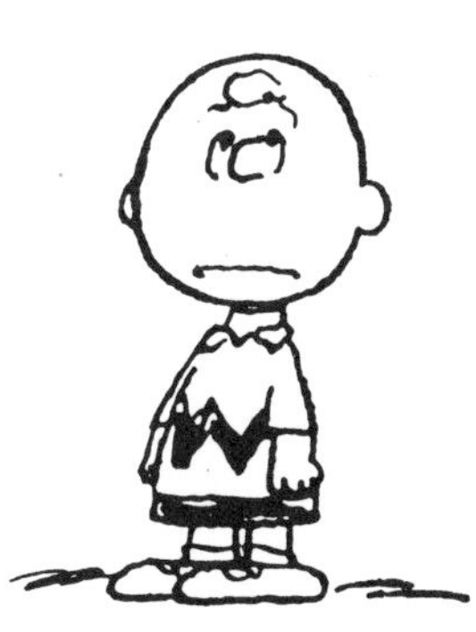

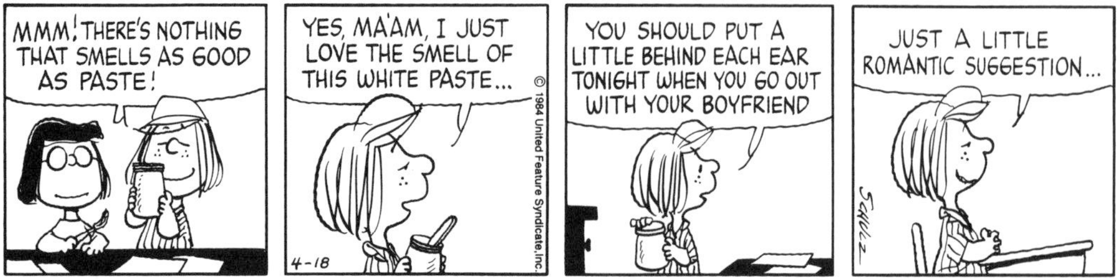
MMM! THERE'S NOTHING THAT SMELLS AS GOOD AS PASTE!
YES, MA'AM, I JUST LOVE THE SMELL OF THIS WHITE PASTE...
© 1984 United Feature Syndicate, Inc.
4-18
YOU SHOULD PUT A LITTLE BEHIND EACH EAR TONIGHT WHEN YOU GO OUT WITH YOUR BOYFRIEND
JUST A LITTLE ROMANTIC SUGGESTION...
SCHULZ

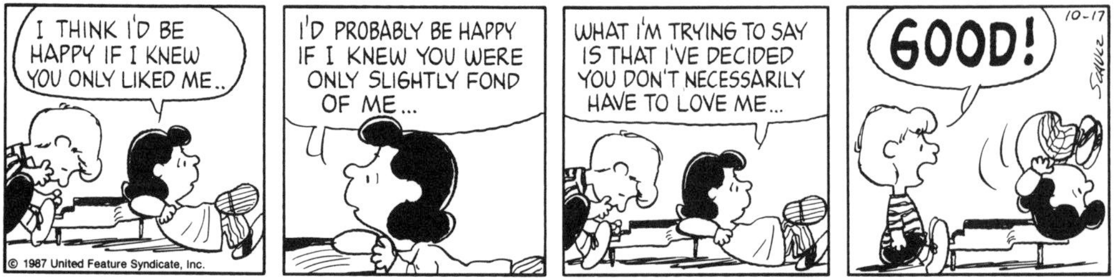
I THINK I'D BE HAPPY IF I KNEW YOU ONLY LIKED ME..
© 1987 United Feature Syndicate, Inc.
I'D PROBABLY BE HAPPY IF I KNEW YOU WERE ONLY SLIGHTLY FOND OF ME...
WHAT I'M TRYING TO SAY IS THAT I'VE DECIDED YOU DON'T NECESSARILY HAVE TO LOVE ME...
GOOD!
10-17
SCHULZ

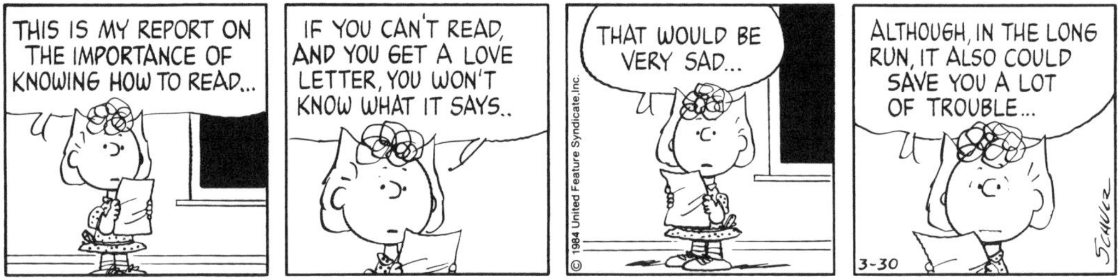
THIS IS MY REPORT ON THE IMPORTANCE OF KNOWING HOW TO READ...
IF YOU CAN'T READ, AND YOU GET A LOVE LETTER, YOU WON'T KNOW WHAT IT SAYS..
© 1984 United Feature Syndicate, Inc.
THAT WOULD BE VERY SAD...
ALTHOUGH, IN THE LONG RUN, IT ALSO COULD SAVE YOU A LOT OF TROUBLE...
3-30
SCHULZ

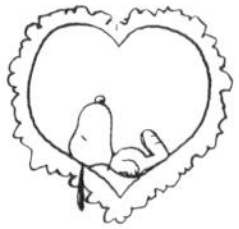

SNOOPY, THE ROMANCE AUTHOR

"Do you love me?" she asked.

"Of course," he said.

"Do you really love me?" she asked.

"Of course," he said.

"Do you really love me?" she asked.

"No," he said.

"Do you love me?" she asked.

"Of course," he said.

So she asked no more.

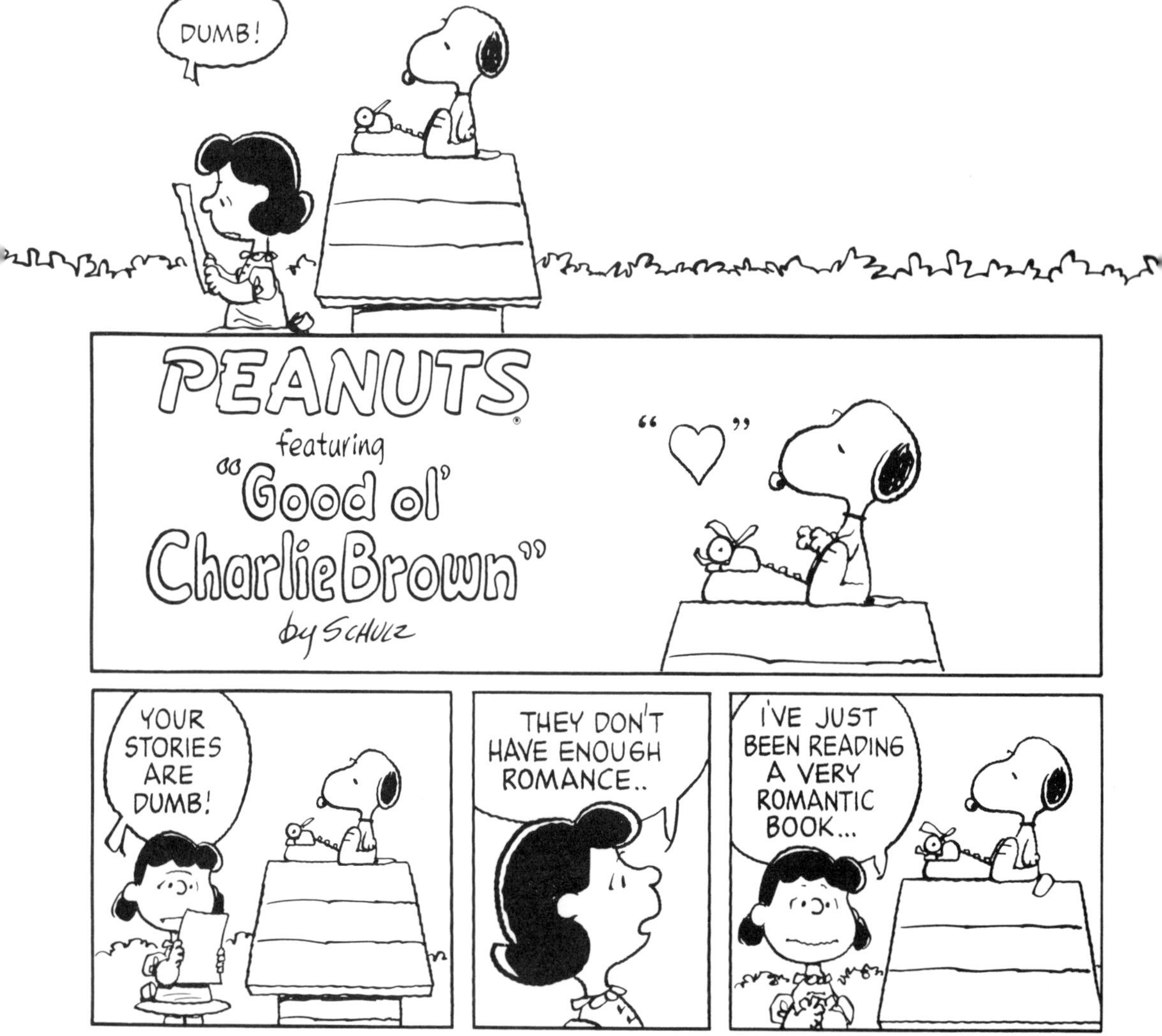
DUMB!
PEANUTS
featuring
"Good ol' Charlie Brown"
by SCHULZ
"♥"
YOUR STORIES ARE DUMB!
THEY DON'T HAVE ENOUGH ROMANCE..
I'VE JUST BEEN READING A VERY ROMANTIC BOOK...

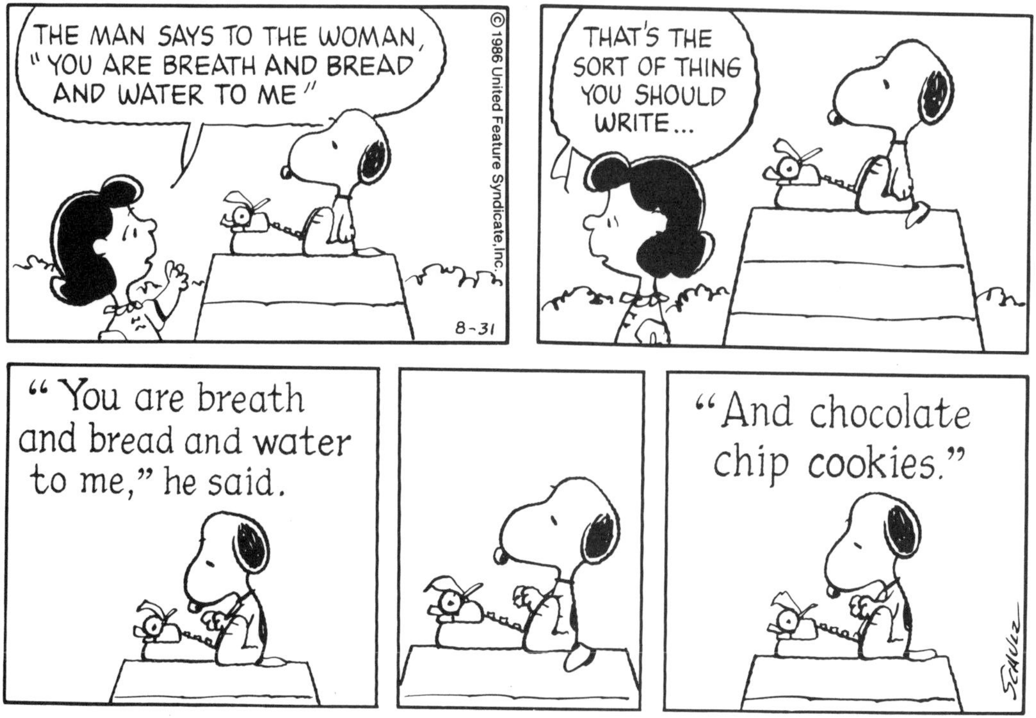
THE MAN SAYS TO THE WOMAN, "YOU ARE BREATH AND BREAD AND WATER TO ME"
© 1986 United Feature Syndicate, Inc.
8-31
THAT'S THE SORT OF THING YOU SHOULD WRITE...
"You are breath and bread and water to me," he said.
"And chocolate chip cookies."
SCHULZ

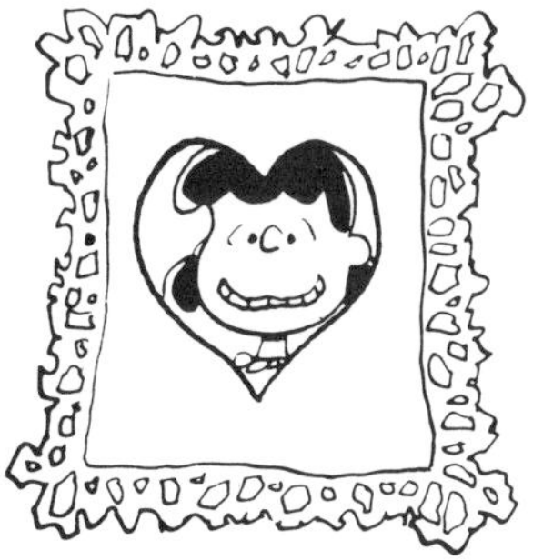

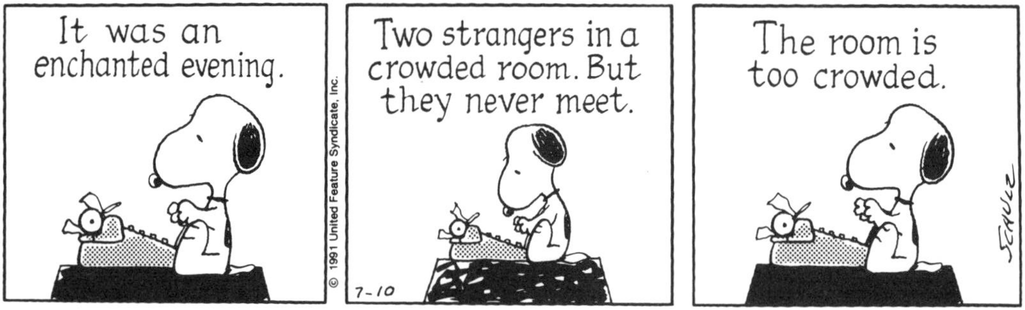
It was an enchanted evening.
© 1991 United Feature Syndicate, Inc.
Two strangers in a crowded room. But they never meet.
7-10
The room is too crowded.
SCHULZ

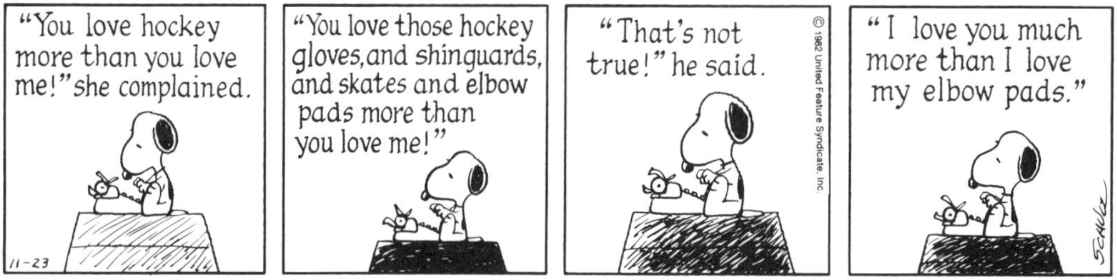
"You love hockey more than you love me!" she complained.
11-23
"You love those hockey gloves, and shinguards, and skates and elbow pads more than you love me!"
"That's not true!" he said.
© 1982 United Feature Syndicate, Inc.
"I love you much more than I love my elbow pads."
SCHULZ

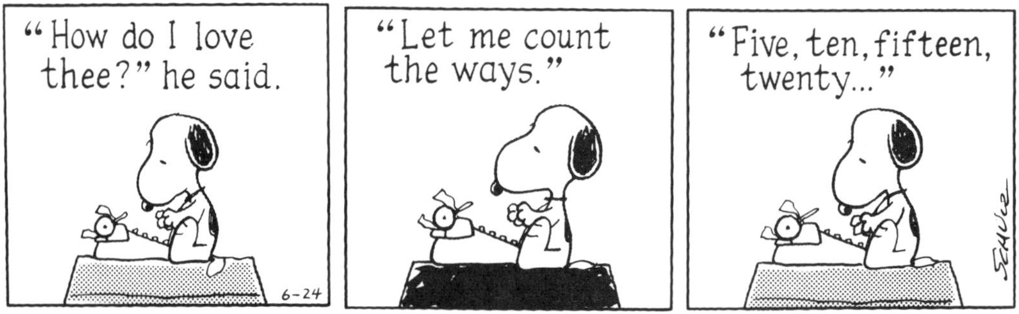
"How do I love thee?" he said.
6-24
"Let me count the ways."
"Five, ten, fifteen, twenty..."
SCHULZ

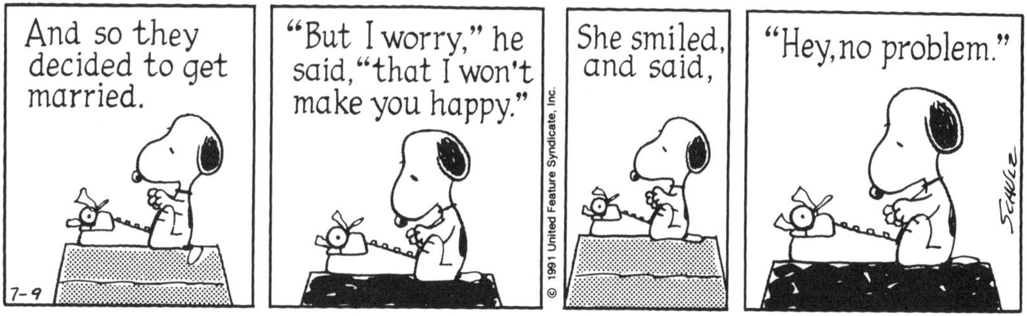
And so they decided to get married.
"But I worry," he said, "that I won't make you happy."
She smiled, and said,
"Hey, no problem."
7-9
© 1991 United Feature Syndicate, Inc.
SCHULZ

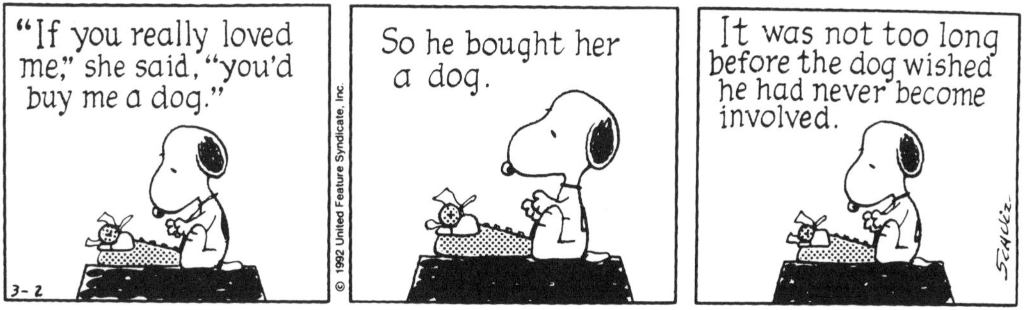
"If you really loved me," she said, "you'd buy me a dog."
So he bought her a dog.
It was not too long before the dog wished he had never become involved.
3-2
© 1992 United Feature Syndicate, Inc.
SCHULZ

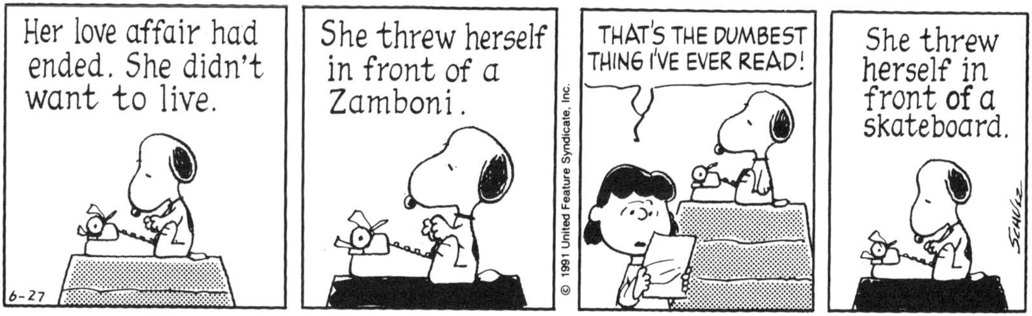
Her love affair had ended. She didn't want to live.
She threw herself in front of a Zamboni.
THAT'S THE DUMBEST THING I'VE EVER READ!
She threw herself in front of a skateboard.
6-27
© 1991 United Feature Syndicate, Inc.
SCHULZ

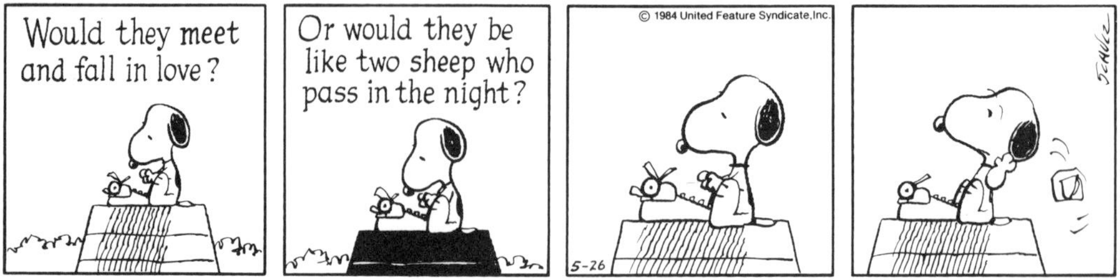
Would they meet and fall in love?
Or would they be like two sheep who pass in the night?
© 1984 United Feature Syndicate, Inc.
5-26
SCHULZ

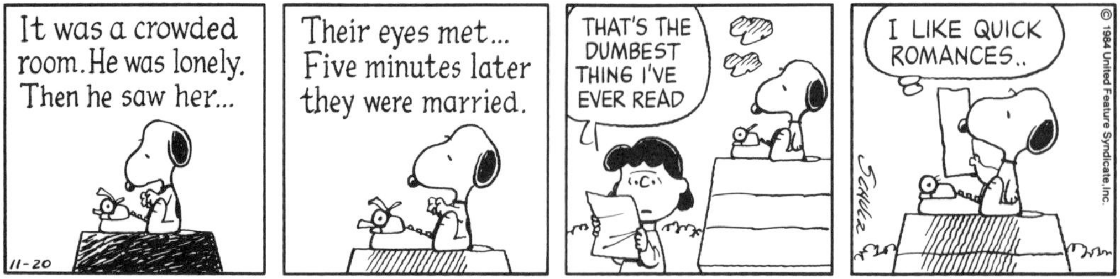
It was a crowded room. He was lonely. Then he saw her...
11-20
Their eyes met... Five minutes later they were married.
THAT'S THE DUMBEST THING I'VE EVER READ
I LIKE QUICK ROMANCES..
SCHULZ
© 1984 United Feature Syndicate, Inc.

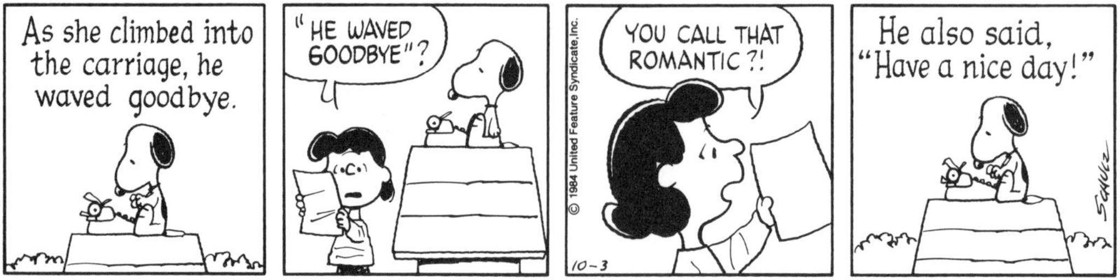
As she climbed into the carriage, he waved goodbye.
"HE WAVED GOODBYE"?
© 1984 United Feature Syndicate, Inc.
YOU CALL THAT ROMANTIC?!
10-3
He also said, "Have a nice day!"
SCHULZ

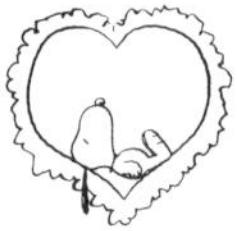